MODULE 8

COMMUNICATING WITH CO-WORKERS

L e a r n e r ' s   G u i d e

*Agency for Instructional Technology
and South-Western Educational Publishing*

ISBN: 0-538-63599-1

Library of Congress Catalog Card Number: 94-66527

1 2 3 4 5 6 7 8 PR 01 00 99 98 97 96 95 94

Printed in the United States of America

I(T)P
International Thomson Publishing

South-Western Educational Publishing
is a division of International Thomson Publishing, Inc.
The ITP trademark is used under license.

Communication 2000 Credits

Agency for Instructional Technology Staff

Mardell Raney—Senior Editor and Art Director

Dr. Alan Backler—Instructional Designer

Dr. David Gudaitis—Executive Producer

John Pesta—Editor and Features Writer

David Strange—Computer Designer/Compositor

Amy Bond—Administrative Assistant

Connie Williamson—Administrative Assistant

Frank Batavick—Director of Projects and New Products

South-Western Educational Publishing Staff

Laurie Wendell—Production Editor/Project Coordinator

Dr. Carolyn Love—Marketing Manager

Elaine St. John-Lagenaur—Senior Designer

Carol Sturzenberger—Production Manager

Michael Draper—Assistant Advertising Manager

South-Western Manufacturing Department

Peter McBride—Vice President/Editor-in-Chief

Project Staff

Margaret C. Albert, President, Matrix Communications Associates, Pittsburgh, PA—Senior Writer

Rhonda Rieseberg—Writer and Features Writer/Editor

Margaret C. Albert, Mark Doremus, Ken Goodall, Mary Ellen Matthews, Rhonda Rieseberg, Judy Sheese, Lee Wood—Module Writers

Dana Lundell, Anne Parks, Jan Raabe—Literature Lesson Writers

Brenda Grannan, Joe Lee, Maureen Pesta—Literature Illustrations

Brenda Grannan—Cover Designs and Internal Graphics

Dave Coverly—Cartoons

Jeff Deuser, Karla Dunn, Wesley Raabe—Assistant Compositors

Brad Bloom—Permissions

Jim Shea—Project Evaluator/Developer of Student Assessment

Video and Audio Production

Bob Risher—Script Writer

Brad Bloom and Amy Crowell—Assistant Producers

Bill Crawford—Logo Design (print and video)

John McGibbon—Off-Line Editor

David Yosha—Director/Videographer

The Quantum Group—On-Line Editing

Mark Doremus—Barcode Technician

Lodestone Productions—Producers, Literature on Tape

Content Consultants for *Communication 2000*

Dr. Patricia Andrews, Professor of Speech Communication, Indiana University (Speaking and Listening)

Dr. Richard Beach, Professor of English Education, University of Minnesota (Literature)

Dr. Rebecca Burnett, Professor of English, Iowa State University (Technical Writing)

Dr. Daniel Callison, Professor of Library and Information Science, Indiana University (Information Literacy)

Dr. Julie Miller, Counselor and Consultant, Worthington, Ohio (Student Assessment)

Dr. Darryl Strickler, Consultant, Center for Professional Education, Arthur Anderson and Company, St. Charles, Illinois (Reading and Writing)

Special Consultants to South-Western Educational Publishing

Larry P. Bond—Assistant Superintendent for Curriculum and Instruction, Wythe County Schools (Whytheville, VA)

Dr. Willard R. Daggett—Director, International Center for Leadership in Education, Inc. (Schenectady, NY); Author, *Your Future: Plans and Choices*, *The Dynamics of Work*, and *Electronic Office Systems*

Dorothy J. Hoover—Teacher of English, Journalism, and Alternative Education, Huntingdon Area School District (Huntingdon, PA)

Christine B. LaRocco—*Applied Communication* Trainer and Consultant; former English teacher (Boise, ID) Author, *The Art of Work: An Anthology of Workplace Literature*

Jim Coughlin—English teacher, Capital City H.S. (Boise, ID)

(continued on page iv)

Communication 2000 **Credits** (continued)

Reviewers

Kenneth Brown, Consultant, former English teacher
(Eaton Park, FL)

Pauline Buis, English teacher, Ozark H.S. (Ozark, AL)

Linnea LoPresti, Business English, Assistant Dean of
Instruction, Genessee Community College (Batavia, NY)

Jane Miller, English teacher, McKenzie Career Center
(Indianapolis, IN)

Darlene Viele, English teacher, Pembroke H.S. (Corfu, NY)

Michelle Walker, English teacher, Roseburg H.S.
(Roseburg, OR)

Sales Advisory Team

Dick Arculin, Tricia Bobst, Pat Bryzcki, Dave Morgan,
Bob Shaw, Mark Urbanski

Field Evaluators

Bill and Michelle Walker (Roseburg, Or)

Brenda Harmon (St. Cloud, FL)

Lynn Lazarra (Westfield, IN)

Mary Ann Chamberlain (Syracuse, NY)

Linda Holmstrom (Georgetown, TX)

Focus Groups

Bloomington, IN	Cincinnati, OH
Phyllis Clapacs	Muriel L. Cunningham
Sherry Selph-Judah	Nancy Barker
Shirley Pugh	Mary Kathleen Barger
LadyAnn Loudenback	Lillian A. Hawkins
Barbara Grady	Beth M. Harding
Lori Hoevener	Jane Vera Lemker
	Connie L. Robinson
	Doris J. Riddle
	James E. Swift
	Robert West

The South-Western Educational Publishing staff salutes the
dedicated professionals at the Agency for Instructional
Technology for their tireless efforts and ongoing commitment to excellence in education.

Contents

Introduction

What do you need to succeed in the working world? The ability to work hard, solve problems, and do your part as a team member is a good start. But even with your best efforts, you will still need the one thing all employers look for as they hire the work force for the 21st century: good communication skills. Your preparation for the working world of tomorrow begins today with *Communication 2000,* a multimedia course that will help you develop the reading, writing, listening, and speaking skills necessary to get and keep a job.

Module 8 of *Communication 2000* focuses on the skills you will need to communicate effectively with co-workers and supervisors. Your ability to give—and follow—directions, adapt to others' communication styles, present your point of view, and avoid language traps will lead to greater opportunities on and off the job. As you complete the activities, view the video, and practice the strategies of Module 8, you will

- see the behind-the-scenes pressures that affect communication at the Sci-Fi Channel.

- test your ability to give—and follow—directions.

- learn how the U.S. government can search its $50 million monthly phone bill in seconds.

- catch the dream that energized America in the 1960s.

- consider strategies for negotiating on an uneven playing field.

Communicating at Work

A Video Lesson

Looking Ahead

What This Lesson Is About

In this lesson, you will learn about the importance of communicating effectively with co-workers and supervisors in the workplace.

✔ Today's workplace increasingly calls for employees who are skilled in spoken and written communication.

✔ Good communication skills help you interact with co-workers to make decisions, resolve conflicts, solve problems, and get the promotion you want.

✔ These skills also help you relate to your supervisors, who guide you in carrying out your tasks and meeting your goals.

On-the-job communication can be improved when employees have respect for each other, regardless of their positions.

1

Key Ideas

communication skill—the ability to read, write, listen, and speak effectively while performing tasks

co-worker—a person with whom you work

oral communication—a spoken message

supervisor—a worker who is in charge of other workers

written communication—a typed, handwritten, printed, e-mailed, or faxed message

Viewing the Videodisc—Introduction

You are about to see the first videodisc or videocassette segment about communicating with co-workers and supervisors.

As you watch the segment, ask yourself,

"How do good communication skills help employees interact with their co-workers and supervisors?"

Post-Viewing Questions

After you have watched the video segment, answer the following questions:

1 Which communication skills are important for working with co-workers? Why do you say so?

2 How can your communication skills affect your relationships with co-workers? Give examples.

3 What advice did you hear about dealing with supervisors? Do you agree? Why or why not?

Be prepared to share your answers with the class.

Introduction

Search 329, Play To 5359

Introduction: Discussion Question 1

Search Frame 5360

Introduction: Discussion Question 2

Search Frame 5361

Introduction: Discussion Question 3

Search Frame 5362

"You'll spend eight hours a day with them. Working, sharing, communicating. Your co-workers will be very important people in your life."

2

Getting Started

The Changing Workplace

Today's workplace increasingly involves the exchange of oral and written communication with supervisors and co-workers. More and more companies are empowering workers to make decisions and are turning to teamwork to get jobs done. This calls for workers with good communication skills. In addition, more and more jobs involve working with computers or other technologically advanced machinery—and this too requires good communication skills.

It's not very enjoyable to perform a job where you merely take orders from the boss and do the same thing over and over. That's how most jobs were handled during the industrial age, back when your grandparents and great-grandparents first went to work.

These days, in a wide range of occupations, the situation has changed. The new corporate style for the age of computers, faxes, phones, and e-mail is employee empowerment. This business philosophy places more responsibility and the potential for power in the hands of employees. Employee empowerment lets workers make decisions, solve problems, and resolve conflicts on their own. It makes jobs more enjoyable and more challenging than they used to be.

This new corporate style makes communication skills vitally important. In these new environments, you must be able to receive and send written and spoken messages effectively. Having good communication skills helps you solve workplace problems, avoid making mistakes, and be considered for promotion. Communication skills also help you work with your supervisors in carrying out your tasks and achieving your goals—and they can keep you on good terms with your supervisors and co-workers.

On a separate piece of paper, answer this question:

- Why is it important for today's workers to know how to communicate effectively?

Be prepared to share your answer with the class.

Trying It Out

Viewing the Videodisc—Sci-Fi Channel

In the next videodisc segment, you will watch a highly creative group of employees working at the Sci-Fi Channel in New York.

As you watch the segment, ask yourself,

"How important is effective communication at the Sci-Fi Channel?"

Sci-Fi Channel

Search 5369, Play To 14471

3

Post-Viewing Questions

After you have watched the video segment, answer the following questions:

1 Why is communication among co-workers critical to the success of the Sci-Fi Channel?

2 What advice does Sandy give for communicating with co-workers and supervisors? How does that compare to your own experience?

3 According to Ken, how do the employees at the Sci-Fi Channel resolve disagreements?

Be prepared to share your answers with the class.

"You also have to understand that your co-workers aren't against you— they're on your side. You can speak frankly, but don't be harsh," says Sandy Dean, associate producer at the Sci-Fi Channel.

Summing Up

Newshound

Imagine that you are a reporter for a television industry newspaper. Your boss gives you an assignment to write a feature story on the ways that good communication skills help in the creation of TV productions. (A feature story focuses on an interesting person or topic. Unlike a news story, whose purpose is to report the latest events, a feature can be written in a more casual, entertaining style.) You visit the Sci-Fi Channel, watch its employees at work, and interview several of them.

On a separate piece of paper, write a feature story of six or seven paragraphs based on the idea that good communication skills are valuable in today's workplace. Illustrate this idea by reporting one or two ways in which the Sci-Fi Channel's supervisors and co-workers use effective communication to perform their jobs. Base your story on actions and quotations from the video segment. Assume that the workers' comments in the segment were made to you during personal interviews. You may wish to watch the segment again and to take notes before you write.

Be prepared to share your feature story with the class.

Keeping Track

On a separate piece of paper, answer the following questions. Use what you have learned in this lesson to help you.

1 Why are communication skills becoming more and more important in today's workplace?

2 How can communication skills help you interact with your co-workers?

3 Why are communication skills important in relating to supervisors?

Company Profile

Company Name: Sci-Fi Channel

Location: New York, New York

Mission Statement:
"The Sci-Fi Channel (SFC) is a specialty cable-television network dedicated to science fiction, horror, and fantasy programming."

Company Products and/or Services:
"Our programming lineup consists of series, movies, specials, and originally produced movies and shows"

Clients and Customers:
"The Sci-Fi Channel is seen in 16.5 million homes in the United States."

Number of Employees:
53 who work solely for SFC, plus others who work for both SFC and USA Networks

Unique Features:
"We are the only network devoted exclusively to sci-fi, horror, and fantasy."

5

Going Further

- In the first video segment in this lesson, Paula Brown, who is vice president of creative services for USA Networks, gives this advice on how to work with other persons:

  > If they like to do things in written form, learn how to write memos. If they're on the phone constantly, call them on the phone. If they drop by your office 20 times a day, drop by their office. You're going to be most effective not by communicating to them in your chosen style, but figuring out what is their chosen style. It's like learning their language.

  Write a brief explanation of why you agree or disagree with Paula Brown's advice. Try to illustrate your argument with examples drawn from your own experiences with other students in school or with co-workers on a job.

  Be prepared to share what you write with your classmates and teacher.

- In the second video segment in this lesson, Ken Krupka, manager of on-air promotion for the Sci-Fi Channel, makes this statement about the employees he supervises:

  > We have an awful lot of creative talent involved, and sometimes egos get in the way. So I try to keep things as positive as possible. We also are very much open to ideas. There's no such thing as a bad idea. I'm open to all ideas. So we have a lot of open communication.

  Write a few paragraphs telling why you would or would not like to work for a supervisor like Ken Krupka.

  Be prepared to share what you write with your classmates and teacher.

"To succeed in the work force, you need problem-solving, quantitative, reasoning, and oral and written skills. You also need the ability to communicate with people at your level, and those below and above you. The way you do your work may change, and you may have to adapt to new technology, but your ability to change will be enhanced if you have these basic skills."

—Ronald E. Kutscher, associate commissioner, Bureau of Labor Statistics, U.S. Department of Labor

Supervisor and Employee Interaction

A Concept Lesson

Looking Ahead

What This Lesson Is About

In this lesson, you will learn why communication among supervisors and employees is more important today than it ever has been. Good communication skills make employees more productive and more valuable to supervisors and employers.

✔️ Relationships between supervisors and employees are changing. Less emphasis is being placed on a command and control system.

✔️ Yesterday's workplace often sought employees who would simply follow instructions.

✔️ In many of today's workplaces, however, employees are asked to anticipate problems and to solve them creatively.

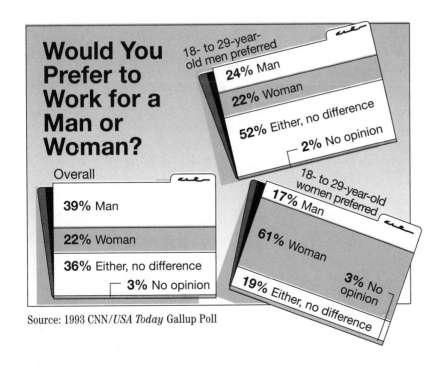

Would You Prefer to Work for a Man or Woman?

18- to 29-year-old men preferred
- **24%** Man
- **22%** Woman
- **52%** Either, no difference
- **2%** No opinion

Overall
- **39%** Man
- **22%** Woman
- **36%** Either, no difference
- **3%** No opinion

18- to 29-year-old women preferred
- **17%** Man
- **61%** Woman
- **3%** No opinion
- **19%** Either, no difference

Source: 1993 CNN/*USA Today* Gallup Poll

Terminal Trouble

You are working at a truck terminal loading freight for Tuffluck Trucking Company. Your boss, Eagle Beekman, keeps a tight rein on everything. He keeps a close eye on you and the other dock workers to make sure no one "goofs off," as he puts it. He becomes verbally abusive if a worker clocks in late, and he demands that workers follow his instructions to the letter.

Tuffluck Trucking has detailed rules about how the work is to be done, and boss Beekman permits no deviation from the rules. He decides everything—when, where, and how the work will be done and who will do it.

Yet despite the rules and Beekman's prodding, the work seldom gets finished on time. You and the other dock workers feel resentful and angry. Some of the rules seem to be counterproductive. The team works slowly, doing just enough to get by, and the truckers often must wait extra hours to pick up their loads. You see ways the bottlenecks might be eliminated, but Beekman won't listen to your ideas. You have given up trying to talk to him. You and the other workers no longer care whether Tuffluck succeeds or fails.

On a separate piece of paper, answer the following questions:

1 What do you think is wrong with supervisor-employee relations at Tuffluck Trucking? Does the fault lie with the workers, with the managers, or with both?

2 How can supervisor-employee interaction at Tuffluck be improved?

Be prepared to share your answers with the class. Save them for possible use later in this lesson.

Increased sensitivity to employee relations was one factor leading to the dramatic recovery of American productivity by 1993. According to a study by the McKinsey Global Institute, American manufacturing companies that year led Japan in productivity by 17 percent and Germany by 21 percent. A report based on the study also showed that American workers were more efficient than Japanese workers in four of nine industries and more productive than German workers in seven of nine industries.

—Adapted from Sara Collins, "Business: America Cranks It Up," *U.S. News & World Report* (March 28, 1994).

Getting Started

A Breakdown in Relations

In the late 1970s, after years of steady improvement, worker productivity in the United States took a nosedive. Many owners and managers blamed employees for the decline. "Young people just don't want to work anymore," some said.

But a few experts had a different explanation. They blamed the decline in productivity on a lack of understanding and cooperation between workers and management. Some said the villain was an outdated system of employee relations that had grown up with the industrial revolution, which began in the 18th century. Such a system just wasn't working in this age of high technology.

Many companies have taken seriously the criticism of their employee relations. Getting rid of their old ways, they are asking employees to be more proactive—that is, to speak up when they see problems developing and to work in teams to solve these problems. Many companies are also asking their employees to be more creative—to find ways to do their jobs better, quicker, and cheaper.

In progressive firms like these, top executives establish broad goals and objectives, then they ask teams of workers to decide

9

how these goals will be achieved. In this way, they are empowering employees to take responsibility for their own success.

Employee empowerment requires effective two-way communication between employees and managers. In this new kind of workplace, employees do more than follow orders—they interact. They constantly receive and generate information. In such an environment, good listening, speaking, reading, and writing skills are vital to success on the job.

Experts say that today's companies must adopt the new values in worker relations if they hope to survive and prosper in a global high-technology marketplace. That means they need employees who can communicate well. *You* can be one of them.

On a separate piece of paper, answer the following questions:

1 How does the new workplace differ from the scene at Tuffluck Trucking's terminal?

2 Refer to your answers to the questions in the first part of this lesson. How do your thoughts on ways that Tuffluck could improve worker-supervisor interaction compare with the techniques recommended for use in the new workplace?

Be prepared to share your answers with the class.

> *"If something has been done a particular way for fifteen or twenty years, it's a pretty good sign, in these changing times, that it is being done the wrong way."*
>
> —Elliot M. Estes, former G.M. president

Trying It Out

Changing Roles in the Workplace

Not all companies, of course, are team-oriented. Not all employees experience the benefits and demands of problem solving and decision making. Many companies still conduct employee relations as Tuffluck Trucking does.

For a few moments, consider the situation presented in **Terminal Trouble** from the point of view of the boss, Eagle Beekman, and the owners of Tuffluck Trucking. They are acting under the traditional industrial model of workplace relations, with rigid directions or commands coming from the top down.

Think about what the traditional model seeks in an employee. Imagine that you work at Tuffluck and need to hire a new dock worker. Using your copy of the **Changing Employee** form, list in the left-hand column at least four characteristics that you would want a potential worker to have. Then create a help-wanted ad for Tuffluck to run in a newspaper to fill the position.

Now imagine you work at Sun Spirit, an up-and-coming greeting card company that follows the employee empowerment philosophy. You are seeking to hire a new employee for the mailroom. Again, using your copy of the **Changing Employee** form, list in the right-hand column at least four characteristics that you would seek in a potential worker. Then create a help-wanted ad for Sun Spirit to run in a newspaper.

Be prepared to share your lists of characteristics and your ads with the class.

Summing Up

Bringing Tuffluck Up to Speed

Employees in today's workplace are finding new opportunities to contribute ideas and to solve problems. While not all companies embrace the idea of employee participation, industry leaders have moved in that direction. To work for these top companies, employees must have good communication skills.

Imagine that the owners of Tuffluck Trucking Company have decided to make changes. For one thing, they intend to change the name to Goodluck. They also plan to computerize the loading operations. More important, they want to improve employee relations, and they have hired an expert—you—to assist them.

Develop a plan for improving supervisor-employee interaction and for bettering employee relations at the new Goodluck Trucking.

Be prepared to present your plan to the class.

> *"Change is happening faster than we can keep tabs on and threatens to shake the foundations of the most secure American business."*
> —U.S. Congress Office of Technology

The Changing American Work Force

- In 1950, the American work force was 60 percent unskilled workers and 40 percent skilled and professional/managerial workers.

- In 1992, the American work force was 65 percent unskilled workers and 35 percent skilled and professional/managerial workers.

- By the year 2000, the estimated American work force will be 15 percent unskilled workers and 85 percent skilled and professional/managerial workers.

What do these trends mean to you?

—Data from Bureau of Labor Statistics, U.S. Department of Labor

Changing Employee

Traditional Workplace	New Workplace
Characteristics of Worker	**Characteristics of Worker**
1.	1.
2.	2.
3.	3.
4.	4.
Help Wanted	**Help Wanted**

Keeping Track

On a separate piece of paper, answer the following questions. Use what you have learned in this lesson to help you develop your answers.

1 What form does supervisor-employee interaction often take in traditional workplaces?

2 What form does supervisor-employee interaction often take in today's workplace?

3 Why are good communication skills particularly useful for employees today?

The Trend in Trucking

The Bureau of Labor Statistics has projected that 410,000 new trucking industry jobs would be created from 1990 to 2005, with employment rising from 1.6 million to 2 million.

Going Further

■ Schedule a visit, either in person or by phone, with the personnel manager or a supervisor who interviews potential employees at a local firm. Find out what general characteristics the company looks for in new employees. Take notes as you listen. After the interview, determine whether the firm has entered the new age of worker-supervisor interaction. Be prepared to report your findings to the class and your teacher.

■ As you watch television news programs and read newspapers and magazines, look for examples of new types of company-worker relations. Keep a log of examples, and imagine what it would be like to work in the situations that you find. Write a paragraph about one example, and be prepared to share it with the class and your teacher.

■ Management consultant Tom Peters writes and lectures about the need for companies to adapt to changing conditions. Find examples of new kinds of company-worker relations in his books, for example *The Tom Peters Seminar: Crazy Times Call for Crazy Organizations* (New York: Vintage, 1994). Briefly summarize one of his examples. Be prepared to share it with the class and your teacher.

Change

We live in a time of paradox, contradiction, opportunity, and above all, change. To the fearful, change is threatening because they worry that things may get worse. To the hopeful, change is encouraging because they feel things may get better. To those who have confidence in themselves, change is a stimulus because they believe one person can make a difference and influence what goes on around them. These people are the doers and the motivators.

—Buck Rogers,
Getting the Best Out of Yourself & Others

Both tears and sweat are salty, but they render a different result. Tears will get you sympathy, sweat will get you change.

—Jesse Jackson,
American civil rights leader

Progress is a nice word. But change is its motivator and change has its enemies.

—Robert F. Kennedy,
former U.S. Attorney General

Daily Routine

A Literature Lesson

Looking Ahead

What This Lesson Is About

In this lesson, you will read a poem called "Shifting Piles." It describes a worker's routine that appears to offer little satisfaction and little interaction with co-workers. The poet uses rhyme, alliteration, and repetition to create a particular effect.

✔ Doing repetitive tasks that limit communication with supervisors and co-workers can lead to boredom in the workplace.

✔ Workers who find themselves in such situations may use imaginative ways to cope with them.

✔ For some persons, creative writing can be a way both to tell about and to relieve the effects of these situations.

Key Ideas

alliteration—the repetition of consonant sounds that begin words, for example "wet, windy weekend"

boredom—the state of being weary, restless, and uninterested

creative—imaginative; being able to produce something or make something happen by using imaginative skills

narrator—the person or character who tells a story or provides commentary on it

repetitive—repeated over and over

rhyme—the repetition of sounds that end words, for example "a mouse in a house"

routine—a repetitive procedure for performing a task

tone—a particular mood or attitude in writing or speech

I'm Bored!

Recall a time when you were performing a task at home or at work that made you feel really bored—so bored that you couldn't stand it any longer and had to give up on the task. Being as specific as possible, write an entry in your journal answering the following questions:

1 How would you describe that boring task?

2 Why did the task bore you? How did you feel about it?

3 What happened when you gave up on the task?

Keep your journal entry handy for use later in this lesson.

Getting Started

"Shifting Piles" by Lesléa Newman

As you read the following selection, pay close attention to the poem's word and sound patterns—its **rhyme** (words such as "piles" and "files"), **alliteration** (such as "pile" and "pull"), and **repetition**. Note how the repetitive wording and repetitive sounds create a certain effect. The words and sounds seem to reflect the work environment and to express the attitude and feelings of the narrator—the worker in the poem. The tone of the poem mimics both the setting and the worker's feelings.

Jot down on a separate piece of paper the words and sounds that you feel contribute to the overall effect of the poem.

Brenda Grannan

Shifting Piles

I place a pile of credits to my left
and a pile of debits to my right.
After I type the numbers from the debits
onto the credits
I pile the debits on top of the credits.
Then I pull the carbons from the credits
and separate the copies into piles.
I interfile the piles
and bring them over to the files
where I file the piles and pull the files
making a new file of piles.
Then I make files
for the pile that has no files
and put them into a new file pile.
I take the new file pile down the aisle
over to the table where Mabel
makes labels for April to staple.
I take the new labeled stapled file pile
back down the aisle over to the file
to be interfiled with the pile of filed files.
After I file April's piles
I get new debits from Debby
and new credits from Kerry.
I carry Kerry's credits and Debby's debits
back to my desk
and place a pile of credits to my left
and a pile of debits to my right.
After I type the numbers from the debits
onto the credits
it's 10:00
and we have exactly fifteen minutes
to go down to the cafeteria
and drink coffee
or go out into the parking lot
and scream.

Newman, Lesléa. "Shifting Piles," from "Adjustments" in _Love Me Like You Mean It_, ©1987, 1993 by Lesléa Newman. Published by Clothespin Fever Press. Reprinted by permission of the author.

Mary Vazquez

Meet Lesléa Newman

Before she became a full-time writer, Lesléa Newman worked as a secretary, waitress, day-care teacher, sales clerk, and administrative assistant. Her work history is a good example of the fact that persons who want to be writers must often find other ways to support themselves until their literary endeavors start to sell. Writing talent is not always recognized right away.

Ms. Newman now has 16 books to her credit, including _Secrets_, _Writing from the Heart_, and _In Every Laugh a Tear_. She has received the Highlights for Children Fiction Writing Award, the James Baldwin Award for Cultural Achievement, and other literary honors.

She lives in Massachusetts.

debit—a record of something, such as an amount of money, that is owed

credit—a record of something, such as an amount of money, that has been paid

17

Trying It Out

. . . .

Responding to "Shifting Piles"

After you complete the reading, write your answers to the following questions on a separate piece of paper.

1 Review the words you jotted down. Why do these words stand out? Is it just for their sound, for their meaning, or for both reasons?

2 Why do you think the author chose these particular words? What do they suggest about the feelings of the narrator— the office worker in the poem? What overall tone or attitude do they express?

3 How do these words and phrases affect you as a reader?

4 Look again at the poem's close—the last two lines. What is unusual about these closing lines? What tone or attitude is the worker expressing in these lines? How does this tone differ from the tone expressed in the rest of the poem?

Be prepared to share your answers with the class.

Writing Poetry

Write a short poem about your classroom or work environment. Think about what it's like to be there—the overall atmosphere of the place and the people in it—and how you feel about the situation. Try to mimic this environment through the words you use in your poem, as the author of "Shifting Piles" succeeded in doing. But choose your own tone. Unlike Lesléa Newman, you may want to express happiness, enthusiasm, or some other quality, rather than boredom. Be prepared to share your composition with the class.

Gulp, It's Pulp

A pulper gulps up lots of paper, turns it into glop called pulp, and churns out more paper. How?...

Once paper is collected for recycling, it is sorted by type and color, then it's usually put in a machine called a pulper, which uses water and chemicals to remove ink and other contaminants. The machine turns the paper into a soft, wet material called pulp.

The pulp is sifted through screens that remove staples and other objects. After the pulp is washed, it is usually bleached before being mixed with clean water until it becomes a thick white substance. This is spread into thin layers, heated, dried, and smoothed on a series of rollers, forming new sheets of paper.

Then soon it's back to the pulper again.

18

Summing Up

A Creative Solution

The author of "Shifting Piles" carefully chooses particular words and sounds, which she repeats over and over in an effort to depict a seemingly uninteresting work situation in an interesting way. We don't know whether the author is describing a situation in which she herself was involved. But her imagination is powerful enough to paint a word picture that allows us to experience the situation the same way the worker in the poem does.

Sometimes the workplace can seem complex and unfriendly, and individuals within it can feel overwhelmed and lost. A person caught in the situation described in "Shifting Piles" might with good reason "go out into the parking lot and scream."

For other persons, writing in a creative way about such situations—as Lesléa Newman has done—can be a way to cope with them. Screaming becomes an imaginative action, not a real one.

Review the journal entry you made at the beginning of this lesson, when you recalled a boring experience that occurred at home or at work. In your journal, rewrite that event—revise the circumstances so that you find a creative way to relieve the boredom and complete the task. Describe your imaginative solution.

Then answer the following questions:

1 How would the changes you made in your story relieve your boredom?

2 How would these changes help you complete the task?

3 Why did you make these particular changes?

Be prepared to share your changes and your answers with the class.

Keeping Track

On another sheet of paper, answer the following questions. Use what you have learned in this lesson to help you.

1 How can rhyme, alliteration, and repetition be used to create a particular effect in a poem? Give some examples.

2 What effect can repetitive tasks have on an employee?

3 What can workers do if they become bored while performing routine tasks?

Going Further

∎ Over the next several days, keep alert to your feelings in your classroom or place of employment. At the end of each day, try to recall one or more tasks that caused feelings of boredom. Write a short description of each task and your feelings about it. Then describe how you did or did not cope with these feelings. In particular, describe any creative ways you found to help you complete the task. Be prepared to share your writing with your class and teacher.

∎ Write a short poem or song based on the journal entries you wrote for this lesson. Try to depict and evoke both the boring situation and your strategy for relieving boredom. Be prepared to share your work with the class.

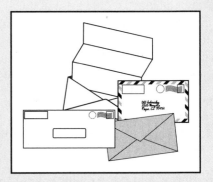

"The U.S. is the world's largest producer of pulp, paper, and paperboard.

With annual sales of $128 billion, it is among the nation's top 10 manufacturing industries....Exports accounted for 60 percent of the growth in paper, paperboard, and market pulp production from 1987 through 1992. Measured another way, exports of these products worldwide increased by a total of 56 percent over the same period."

—Maureen R. Smith, international vice president, American Forest and Paper Association

Following and Giving Oral Instructions

A Strategies Lesson

Looking Ahead

What This Lesson Is About

This lesson focuses on some of the listening and speaking skills that you will need in the workplace. These skills are essential both for following and for giving oral instructions.

☑ When you receive oral instructions, it is useful to screen out distractions, listen actively, seek clarification, and give feedback.

☑ When you follow oral instructions, a good way to proceed is to visualize the task by drawing a flowchart.

☑ When you give oral instructions, a four-part strategy—plan, prepare, deliver, confirm—can be helpful.

You can be sure of numbers, names, and deadlines if you take notes when someone gives you oral instructions.

Key Ideas

feedback—a verbal or nonverbal response from the receiver of a message to the sender, usually to seek clarification or to confirm that the message has been understood

flowchart—a diagram showing the steps in an activity, process, or procedure

Describe and Draw—If You Can!

Here is an activity that will challenge your oral communication skills. Working in pairs, choose to play either the speaker or the listener. Then sit back-to-back so that you can't see each other.

The speaker receives a geometric shape from your teacher and conceals it from the listener. Without describing the shape, the speaker tells the listener how to draw it. The listener, following the instructions as they are given, draws the shape on a piece of paper. The listener must not erase any part of the drawing—once a line is drawn, it must remain.

When you are finished, compare the two drawings. Do they match? If not, what went wrong? Was there a breakdown in communication? What could you do to achieve a closer match next time, without changing the rules? If there is time, switch roles and try it again.

Be prepared to discuss your experience with the class.

Getting Started

Following Oral Instructions

Knowing how to receive and follow the oral instructions of a supervisor or co-worker is important in the workplace, where numerous directions are given every day by word of mouth.

Receiving oral instructions involves being a good listener. To be a good listener, you must first **screen out distractions**. Stop what you're doing; look at the supervisor or co-worker who is talking; and concentrate on what is being said. In many cases, it is a good idea to take notes.

Listen actively. Ask yourself the following questions:

- What is the task I'm being asked to perform?
- What is the desired outcome?
- What steps must be performed, and in what order?
- What will the final product look like?

- How does this task fit in with the things I've already learned or done?

- What existing skills and knowledge can I apply here?

Seek clarification. If you don't understand the instructions that are being given to you, ask the speaker to clarify them right away. The speaker won't know you don't understand unless you ask.

Give feedback. When the speaker is finished, summarize what was said in your own words. Say, "Okay, this is what you want me to do…." Then repeat the instructions as you understand them. This feedback allows you to confirm that you understand the message.

After you receive your instructions—and before you carry them out—review your notes. Seek more information if you need it. Then visualize how the task should be performed.

To **visualize the task**, it may be helpful to draw a sketch or a flowchart of the process involved in following the instructions. You can think of this flowchart as a "job aid" for following directions. Shown here is a flowchart for the instructions given in **Describe and Draw—If You Can!**

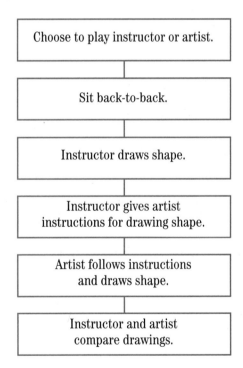

Choose to play instructor or artist.

Sit back-to-back.

Instructor draws shape.

Instructor gives artist instructions for drawing shape.

Artist follows instructions and draws shape.

Instructor and artist compare drawings.

> *"When you stop learning, stop listening, stop looking and asking questions, always new questions, then it is time to die."*
> —Lillian Smith, American writer

Giving Oral Instructions

Supervisors or co-workers often give instructions orally rather than in writing. An oral approach works best when the information is simple or familiar. If the information is complex, put it in writing.

Giving spoken instructions is appropriate when the information must be communicated to a small number of people and does not need to be kept for future reference. The face-to-face setting also allows for instant feedback.

Many people use a four-step approach—plan, prepare, deliver, confirm—when giving oral instructions in the workplace.

1 Before giving instructions, **plan** your presentation. Ask yourself, "What should my co-workers be able to do after I've given these directions?" The answer to this question helps identify your goal or objective. Also do an analysis of your audience. Ask yourself, "How much do my co-workers already know? What's left for me to add?" You don't need to repeat what your co-workers already know.

2 Next **prepare** to give your instructions. Gather all the information you need to explain the instructions completely. Is there something you still need to learn before issuing the directions? If so, get the answer before you begin.

3 Having planned and prepared, you now **deliver** your instructions. Experienced instructors find the following order useful:

- Tell co-workers how long the instruction session will last.
- State the task or process your co-workers will learn.
- Explain why your instructions are important.
- State any health or safety precautions.
- Go over the required equipment and materials.
- Describe the procedure step-by-step.

4 After you have completed the instructions, **confirm** that you have been understood. Ask your co-workers to repeat the information to you or to perform the task you have just explained. Encourage questions. If necessary, restate your instructions in a new way. Don't just ask, "Does everyone understand?" Many people say they understand even when they don't.

> *"One who never asks either knows everything or nothing."*
>
> —Malcolm Forbes, American publisher

Dial 9-1-1 and Follow Directions

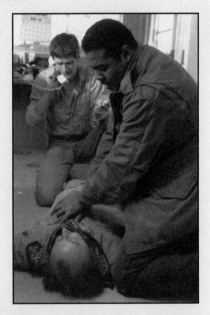

Across the workroom, you happen to see a co-worker struggle to his feet, clutch his left arm, and fall unconscious to the floor. As another co-worker checks for signs of breathing, you grab the nearest phone and dial 9-1-1. Two rings later, a calm 9-1-1 operator answers and begins asking questions and giving you directions. You do your best to repeat the instructions to the worried co-worker who is bending over the still body.

In an emergency at work, you may find yourself having to repeat oral directions to a co-worker. Your ability to listen, understand, and clearly repeat instructions could help save a life.

Other, less life-threatening emergencies occur far more frequently in the workplace. For example, your supervisor may call you with instructions for a co-worker who has a deadline in an hour. Or you may answer a co-worker's phone and be asked to take a detailed message from the company president who has to leave for the airport immediately. When you must repeat oral instructions to someone else, make sure you understand the message first and, if possible, take notes on important names, numbers, or other information.

Trying It Out

Oral Mapping

Work in pairs to practice giving and following oral instructions. If you are the instruction giver, think of a location some distance from school that is familiar to you but not to your partner—for instance, the home or place of employment of someone you know. Develop detailed oral instructions on how to reach this location. Use the techniques outlined in **Giving Oral Instructions** to plan, prepare, deliver, and confirm the directions.

As the instruction follower, listen carefully to the instructions you receive. Use the guidelines outlined in **Following Oral Instructions**. Take notes if necessary. Then draw a flowchart—a map—based on the instructions that you heard, but keep it out of your partner's sight for the time being.

When you are finished, reverse roles and repeat the procedure.

Then look at the maps together, and write your answers to the following questions on a separate piece of paper.

1 Do the maps contain any errors? If so, how did they occur? Who was responsible—the speaker, the listener, or both?

2 How would you avoid making errors if you did the exercise again?

Be prepared to share your experience with the class.

Summing Up

Your Teachers' Techniques

Giving and receiving oral instructions represent a large part of classroom activity. Over the next two days, observe how your teachers give oral directions. Then consider the following question:

- How could you use your teachers' techniques to give oral instructions to your co-workers on a job?

In your journal, answer this question in a few paragraphs. Be prepared to share what you write with the class.

Keeping Track

On a separate piece of paper, answer the following questions. Use what you have learned in this lesson to help you.

1 For the worker who is listening to oral instructions, what are four useful techniques?

2 For the worker who is following oral instructions, what is the purpose of constructing a flowchart?

3 In the instruction-giving strategy presented in this lesson, what does the instruction giver do if the listeners do not understand?

Going Further

■ Recall a time when something went wrong because you failed to follow another person's oral instructions or because someone failed to follow your oral instructions. Write a few paragraphs telling about the experience and how it did or did not change your listening or speaking habits. Be prepared to share your paragraphs with the class and your teacher.

■ In your opinion, what is the single most important recommendation in the section **Following Oral Instructions**? What is the single most important recommendation in the section **Giving Oral Instructions**? Write a few paragraphs defending your answers, and be prepared to read your explanation in class and to turn in your paragraphs to your teacher.

26

Electronic Monitoring

A Decision-Making Lesson

Looking Ahead

What This Lesson Is About

In this lesson, you will look at some conflicts that may arise in the workplace when supervisors monitor employees' e-mail and other electronic communications.

✔ New technology is making it easy for supervisors to watch what their employees do and say.

✔ Sometimes this monitoring or surveillance is done without the employees' knowledge. Employers who do this believe that they have a right to know what their employees are doing.

✔ Some employees think that electronic monitoring violates their right to privacy.

Electronic monitoring at work can make employees feel as though someone is "looking over their shoulder" every time they pick up the telephone or work on the computer.

Electronic Communications Privacy Act

The Electronic Communications Privacy Act of 1986 extends existing privacy guarantees to cover electronic communication. However, it does permit employers to monitor employee use of the employers' electronic communication equipment and systems.

The Electronic Workplace

Computers, telephones, video cameras, and satellite tracking systems have given companies new power to monitor their employees.

- The computers used by clerks and secretaries can report how fast they are typing and how much time they spend on their coffee breaks.

- Some large freight trucks now carry satellite transmitters that tell the company where the trucks are located, how fast they are going, and how many stops the drivers make.

- Telephone systems let supervisors listen in on conversations between telemarketers and customers.

These are only a few examples of how employees are being monitored electronically. It doesn't happen everywhere, but it is becoming much more common as new technologies become available.

Why do you think companies feel that it is necessary for workers to be electronically monitored? How would you react if you were working for a company that instituted electronic monitoring of your job performance? Would you feel comfortable in such a situation, or would you object to it?

In your journal, write brief answers to these questions. State at least three reasons or justifications for your response.

Be prepared to share your response with the class.

Getting Started

A Privacy Issue?

E-mail is a fast, convenient way to send and receive written messages. To use it, you simply type your message into a computer and select the "send" command. The message is then transmitted by computer link or phone line to the computer of your correspondent anywhere in the world.

TECH TIP

According to the government's top electronic information manager, Francis A. McDonough, electronic records, such as phone and fax-billing, e-mail, and computer files, are "very dangerous to the person who creates the record. Think carefully about what you say, and to whom."

To use e-mail, you need a password. A password is a secret code that lets you get into your e-mail account (where your messages are stored in the computer's memory) but keeps other persons out. In the workplace, this system prevents co-workers from reading your mail or sending messages under your name.

But it is possible for your employer to read your e-mail. Companies have a legal right to do this because they own the e-mail system. They say they need to screen e-mail to make sure the system is not being abused. They want to know whether employees are wasting time sending personal messages or telling jokes. And they want to know whether employees are sharing information that is supposed to be confidential.

Some employees think they have a right to privacy on an e-mail system. Because they have secret passwords, they feel the accounts belong to them and should not be examined without their knowledge and permission.

When it comes to electronic eavesdropping in the workplace, what's fair and what isn't? In the story you are about to read, a supervisor has to make a difficult decision. As you read, think about the issue of privacy from both the supervisor's and the employees' viewpoints.

DelMar Washington's Decision

DelMar Washington supervises the design team of Toys 2000, a large manufacturer of futuristic toys for children. During its first five years in business, T2000 has cornered the market on two popular toys: talking dolls that have miniature CD players inside them and racing cars powered by computer chips. Everything the company makes uses state-of-the-art electronics, and at Christmas the latest T-2000 products are always at the top of children's want lists.

Competition heated up as other firms rushed to imitate T2000 products, but this year things reached the boiling point. It's no longer a matter of imitation: Two competitors have brought out products that look very much like T2000's newest models, and they've been hitting the stores before the T2000 toys are even out of the design department. Management is frantic. Del's boss, the vice president for sales and marketing, is convinced that someone in the design department is selling the company's ideas to the competition. "Find out who it is," the supervisor orders Del. "Do whatever it takes to nail this guy. If this keeps up, T2000 will be out of business, and we'll all be out of our jobs."

Del knows that the company's past success was a direct result of the designers' creativity. Over the years he has built a team of people who work closely together, exchanging ideas and helping one another when they are facing deadlines, which is most of the time. His people trust one another, and they trust him as their supervisor. He never "breathes down their necks," and they

> *"If you're doing something for your company on company time, then I suppose the company has the right to look at what you've done. But anything else, including private mail, ought to be totally removed from any eyes but your own. Personally, though, if I had a sensitive communication, which had to be put on the record, I wouldn't want to use e-mail. I'd prefer to put it in a sealed envelope. Very, very heavily sealed."*
>
> —Nat Hentoff, *Village Voice* columnist

appreciate the freedom to experiment that Toys 2000 gives them. He can't believe that any member of his staff would leak information on the new designs, but he has to respond to his boss's order.

He knows that "whatever it takes" means to monitor everything that goes out of his department, and most things go out by e-mail or fax. He also knows that, as a state-of-the-art electronics firm, T2000 has the latest communication equipment, which has the capacity to store and retrieve all messages that employees send.

Because his staff trusts him, no one ever worries about privacy. The designers know that he is not one to snoop. Because of that trust, Del knows that he just might catch the guilty person if he monitors the e-mail and faxes. On the other hand, if he does not discover anything, it might take the heat off his staff.

■ Should Del monitor his staff's outgoing e-mail and fax messages?

> *"The right to be let alone is becoming obsolete."*
> —Harriet Van Horne, American columnist and radio personality

---

Trying It Out

What Should Del Do?

On a separate sheet of paper, write your answer to the preceding question, and give your reasons for the decision that you think Del should make.

Be prepared to share your answer and reasons with the class.

Summing Up

What If?

If you said that Del should go ahead and monitor the e-mail and faxes, would your answer be different:

- if he were also planning to record employees' telephone calls without their knowledge?

- if the company's personnel policy clearly stated that no electronic communications would be monitored without prior notification?

- if the reason for monitoring was to determine the political or social activities of the employees?

If you said that Del should refuse to monitor the e-mail and faxes, would your answer be different:

- if he had been instructed to monitor only one employee, who was under suspicion?

- if the company's personnel policy clearly stated that all electronic communications would be monitored at random by supervisors?

- if the company president had ordered all supervisors—not just Del—to monitor outgoing communications?

Keeping Track

On a separate piece of paper, answer the following questions. Use what you have learned in this lesson to help you.

1 Why has the electronic surveillance of employees become such a hot issue today?

2 Why do some employers believe that they have the right to monitor all of their employees' communications?

3 Why do some employees consider this an invasion of their privacy?

Cases in Point:
Electronic Monitoring and Access

Occasionally, employees will use on-the-job electronic communication in an inappropriate or even illegal manner. Consider the following examples:

■ The Christopher Commission investigation of the Rodney King beating that occurred in Los Angeles in 1992 revealed approximately 700 offensive messages that police officers sent one another.

■ A former vice president of Borland International, a software firm, was charged with giving sensitive company documents to a competitor, Symantec Corporation, a firm that later hired him. An investigation into the corporate MCI mail account of the accused produced evidence that led to a lawsuit against Symantec's president.

■ E-mail messages were one of the principal sources of evidence used against Marine Lieutenant Colonel Oliver North during the 1987 Iran-Contra trial.

31

Going Further

■ What are your legal rights to privacy? Electronic databases store a great deal of information about individuals: credit histories, medical records, arrests and convictions, financial information from tax returns, telephone calls that you have made or received, and even how often you vote. Who can gain access to this information, and under what circumstances? Search your library's databases and indexes for recent articles on the subject. Read at least three articles from different sources to find the answers to these questions (and any other questions you may have), and summarize them in a one- or two-page paper. Be prepared to share with the class what you learn and to turn in your paper to your teacher.

■ In 1949 British author George Orwell published *Nineteen Eighty-Four*, which became one of the most famous futuristic novels ever written. It predicts a world in which "Big Brother" watches everybody's actions by means of a two-way television system. In addition, a whole new language, "Newspeak," has been developed, as Big Brother seeks to control people's thoughts as well. Although the year 1984 is now history, the rapid development of electronic communication and monitoring makes Orwell's predictions even eerier in today's world. Borrow a copy of the book from your library; read it; and then complete one of the following assignments:

• Compare Orwell's 1984 world with contemporary society. Have any of his predictions come true? Are others more believable today than they would have been in 1949? You may want to do a little research on the state of technology in 1949. You can do this either by visiting the library or by talking with an older friend or family member. Ask about television, VCRs, compact disks, cellular telephones, computers, modems, fax machines, and other technology that we take for granted. Write a one- or two-page paper comparing Orwell's fictional world with today's real world.

• Write a science fiction story of your own, set in 2030 (or whatever year you choose). Use what you know about current technology, and free your imagination to describe a world that is as different from life today as Orwell's was from the life he knew in 1949.

Whichever assignment you choose, be prepared to share it with the class and to turn it in to your teacher.

■ Invite local employers to class to discuss electronic monitoring in their work settings. Ask them to discuss how electronic monitoring works in their offices or companies and why it is used.

By 1994 the United States government had converted its million-page-plus monthly phone bill to six CD-ROM discs. Now government agencies attempting to trim the $50 million monthly bill can identify the date, time, and duration of every long-distance call made from hundreds of thousands of federal telephones—in 18 seconds.

Following and Giving Written Instructions

A Concept Lesson

Looking Ahead

What This Lesson Is About

In this lesson, you will learn how to read and write instructions in the workplace. Following and giving written instructions are important everyday activities that promote interaction among supervisors and co-workers.

☑ A step-by-step approach will help you follow written instructions from your supervisor or co-workers.

☑ You can also use a step-by-step approach in writing instructions for your co-workers.

☑ This lesson gives you an opportunity to prepare a set of written instructions for use in an actual work situation.

PAGE 32 FROM BOB'S "I HATE ASPARAGUS" COOKBOOK

33

The New Classmate

Imagine that you have made friends with a new classmate who just transferred from a school in another city. The teacher assigns a research project for the two of you to do together. You ask your new friend to meet you after school at some convenient place, such as the public library. But the student doesn't know how to get there and asks you for directions.

Choose the meeting spot. Then, on a separate piece of paper, write specific directions telling the student the best way to get from your school to the place where you will meet. Don't draw a map—put the instructions in writing.

Be prepared to share your written instructions with the class.

Getting Started

Reading Written Instructions

You read and follow instructions nearly every day. But the process is not necessarily easy or automatic. It involves skills you must learn.

For reading instructions in the workplace, here is a procedure that will help you:

1. **Make sure you have the right instructions.** If you're trying to hook up a piece of RCA equipment, for example, don't use the Sony manual. If you do, you're bound to get confused.

2. **Skim through the instructions.** Ask yourself, "How much of this do I already know?" Later, when you give the instructions a closer reading, you can spend most of your time on the new information.

3. **Read any safety warnings carefully.** When you try out the instructions, observe these precautions.

4. **Check to see if you need additional materials or equipment.** Get everything you need—screwdriver, wires, etc.—before you start your project.

5 **Go back and read the instructions one step at a time.** If the instructions seem complicated, take written notes or highlight key information. Keep your notes handy until you're completely familiar with the equipment or procedure you are learning.

6 **Make sure you understand the instructions.** Try to summarize the instructions to yourself without referring to the text. If you can't explain the directions to yourself, read them again, or look for more written information, or ask your supervisor or co-workers for help.

As a review, jot down, in your own words on a separate piece of paper, the six steps for reading instructions. Then follow these steps both before and during your reading of the steps for *writing* instructions, which begin at the bottom of this page.

When Written Instructions Go Astray

Don't be surprised if you find yourself reviewing instructions written by someone who has learned the English language as a second language. Today more and more American companies are trying to develop, improve, or expand their international business. A colleague in your company's offices in Rome, Italy, may ask you to review instructions for a new product. A co-worker who was recently transferred from the Mexico City office may write installation instructions for a handbook you are compiling. Whatever the situation, you will need to be especially sensitive to the wording of the instructions so that you avoid any misunderstanding.

In *Anguished English,* Richard Lederer provides several examples of instructions that were translated into the English language, with humorous results:

- **At a Budapest zoo:** Please do not feed the animals. If you have any suitable food, give it to the guard on duty.

- **From the brochure of a car rental firm in Tokyo:** When passenger of foot heave in sight, tootle the horn. Trumpet him melodiously at first, but if he still obstacles your passage then tootle him with vigor.

How would **you** rewrite each of these examples to make them appropriate for a brochure in America?

Giving Written Instructions

In the workplace, it is often better to give instructions in written form rather than orally—for example, when the instructions are complicated or unfamiliar, when many employees in many departments need the information, or when the instructions will be needed many times in the future.

If you are writing instructions for co-workers, there are a few basic steps you should follow:

1 **Analyze your audience.** Determine which workers will be reading your instructions, how well they can follow instructions, and how much they already know. These factors will determine your writing level and the amount of information you need to include.

2 **Identify your purpose.** Decide which specific skills or procedures you want your readers to master and how you will determine when they are mastered.

3 **Choose your format.** Decide how to communicate your message. If the instructions are long and involved, you may need to write a manual. For less complicated instructions, write a checklist, a job aid, or a memo.

Formatting Written Instructions

When you format written instructions by hand or on a computer, your instructions will be easier to read and follow if you:

- Use numbered lists to describe a step-by-step process.

- Use bullets with paragraphs to separate different ideas (as in this feature).

- Use plenty of "white space" throughout the instructions by leaving blank lines between numbered items or paragraphs.

- Use an easy-to-read point size. Saving paper by trying to fit two pages of information onto one page will only make your instructions harder to read and follow.

4 **Organize your information.** Create a step-by-step outline or checklist of procedures to include in your instructions.

5 **Write your instructions.** This should be done step-by-step, using your outline or checklist as a guide.

- In your opening section, identify the task you are covering. Explain who performs the task and why it is important. List any required equipment or materials. *Health and safety precautions should be separated from the rest of your text and highlighted so that they won't be overlooked by your readers.*

- Your detailed instructions come next. Give in sequence the steps to be performed. Start each step with a verb— an action word. Include only the details your readers will need. Anticipate and discuss any potential problems. *Highlight key details with headings or with boldface or italic type.*

- Conclude your written instructions by explaining how the finished product should look so that your readers can check their work. Provide a checklist, illustrations, or diagrams whenever they are needed to summarize key information.

- In giving written instructions, it is all right to use jargon, as long as your readers are familiar with the words. But remember that simple, clear, concise writing is best.

6 **Review your first draft.** Check to see that you have included all necessary information and that it is in the correct order. Be sure your instructions are simple, brief, clear, and accurate. Check your grammar, spelling, and punctuation. Ask co-workers to read and test your instructions and to suggest improvements. Revise the draft wherever necessary before making a final version.

7 **Make a final version, distribute it, and follow up on your instructions.** Make a phone call or other personal contact to make sure your information has been received and is understood.

On a separate piece of paper, create a job aid for yourself by outlining these seven steps for giving written instructions. Keep your job aid clear and brief, but make it complete enough so that you can follow it whenever you need to provide instructions in written form.

Be prepared to share your job aid with the class. On the basis of other students' responses, make changes in your job aid as necessary. Keep the job aid for future use.

If the Dish Fits, Wash It

Imagine that you are the manager of a community college cafeteria. You have several student employees who help with the cooking, serving, and cleanup. Every August you must train a new group of workers. You recently received this new set of dishwashing guidelines from the state health department:

Proper Methods for Manual Dishwashing and Sanitizing

A three-compartment N.S.F. approved sink for washing, rinsing, and sanitizing utensils and equipment including an adequate drain board at each end is required at all new installations, and at the time of replacement of old sinks in existing restaurants. In addition, an N.S.F. approved single compartment sink should be located adjacent to the soiled utensil drain board of the three-compartment sink for prewashing. Sizes of each sink compartment must be adequate to permit immersion of at least 50% of the largest utensil used. A complying four-compartment sink with drain boards on each end is also satisfactory.

Scrape, stack, and segregate dishes. Discard chipped dishes, glasses, cups, and stained silverware. Prewash all dishes and utensils in the single compartment or in a well-style garbage disposal unit. If an overhead spray hose is provided, it must be equipped with a backflow preventer.

Wash all utensils, dishes, and silverware in clean, hot water between 110 degrees and 120 degrees Fahrenheit which contains a suitable detergent in the first compartment of the three-compartment sink.

Rinse with clean hot water. Use the middle compartment of the three-compartment sink.

Sanitize (chemically) by submerging utensils, dishes, and silverware for at least two minutes in water with the appropriate concentration of an approved sanitizer which has been placed in the third compartment of the three-compartment sink. *An appropriate sanitation testing kit is also required at each establishment and should be frequently used.* The sanitizer concentration in this sink must be tested after each water change to ensure the proper amount of chemical is being used to effectively destroy pathogens.

After proper cleaning methods have been utilized, clean and sanitary storage of clean dishes and utensils is extremely important. Utensils must always be placed in an inverted position to prevent contamination from dust, spillage, or other similar potential disease causing factors.

Source: Food Sanitation Manual, Wisconsin Division of Health (March 1989)

Using the information in these guidelines, write a set of instructions for manual dishwashing that can be posted at the work site for all employees to follow. Focus on dishwashing only. Some of the information in the guidelines is not related to this task. Part of your assignment is to decide what should be included in the instructions.

In writing the instructions, follow the steps in the job aid that you prepared for yourself from the information in **Giving Written Instructions**.

When you have finished writing, exchange your dishwashing instructions with your classmate. Use a copy of the **Instructions Feedback** form to assess each other's work. Finally, based on the feedback you receive, revise your instructions as necessary.

Be prepared to share your revised instructions with the class. Keep a copy in your portfolio.

Summing Up

You Be the Judge

You have practiced writing directions for an imaginary classmate, writing a job aid for yourself, and writing instructions for cafeteria workers. In all three cases, your main goals were accuracy, clarity, and brevity.

Read the following set of instructions. On a separate piece of paper, write a paragraph explaining why it is or is not a good example of written instructions.

Be prepared to share your critique with the class.

Toaster Use and Care

1. Set toast color adjustment bar to the color of toast desired. Move adjustment bar to the LEFT for light or to the RIGHT for darker toast.

   NOTE: Toast thin-sliced bread on the light toast color control settings.

2. Insert bread and push down lever. When toast is done, it will pop up and current will shut off automatically. Use bread slices that will fit freely into the toaster slots.

3. After constant repeated use, or after changing to a toast setting from pastry, the lever may not lock down in the toasting position. Pause briefly to allow toasting mechanism to cool. It should automatically reset and you may continue toasting.

39

Instructions Feedback

1. Audience and Purpose

Do the instructions tell the dishwashers what they need to know?	☐ Yes	☐ No
Is the language appropriate for the dishwashers' level of understanding?	☐ Yes	☐ No
Do the instructions identify and fulfill their purpose?	☐ Yes	☐ No

2. Content

Do the instructions give all the necessary directions?	☐ Yes	☐ No
Is the information given correctly?	☐ Yes	☐ No
Is the information given simply and briefly?	☐ Yes	☐ No
Is there any unnecessary information?	☐ Yes	☐ No
If health and safety information is needed, is it included and highlighted?	☐ Yes	☐ No

3. Organization

Are any elements missing?	☐ Yes	☐ No
Are the instructions arranged in the correct order?	☐ Yes	☐ No
If a summary diagram would help, is one included?	☐ Yes	☐ No

4. Design

Is the design appropriate for a job aid?	☐ Yes	☐ No
Are the most important words or sentences emphasized appropriately?	☐ Yes	☐ No
Are headings used effectively?	☐ Yes	☐ No
Are useful illustrations included?	☐ Yes	☐ No

5. Clarity

Is the wording clear?	☐ Yes	☐ No
Is the wording accurate?	☐ Yes	☐ No
Is the wording consistent?	☐ Yes	☐ No
Does each instruction begin with an action word?	☐ Yes	☐ No
Are there any unnecessary words?	☐ Yes	☐ No
Did a co-worker test the instructions and find them usable?	☐ Yes	☐ No

6. Grammar, Spelling, and Punctuation

Is the writing grammatically correct?	☐ Yes	☐ No
Are there any errors in spelling or punctuation?	☐ Yes	☐ No

40

Keeping Track

On a separate piece of paper, answer the following questions. Use what you have learned in this lesson to help you.

1 In reading instructions in the workplace, what should you do if you can't understand the directions?

2 In giving written instructions, why is it important to review your first draft?

3 Why is it important, when giving written instructions, to leave out unnecessary information?

Going Further

■ Find five examples of written instructions in your classroom or school—in textbooks, on signs giving directions at entrances or in hallways, in rules for students and teachers, and elsewhere. Record your finds on your copy of the **Checklist of Instructions** form. In the left-hand column, list the location where you found each set of instructions. Use the second column to note the instructions' format (book, manual, job aid, checklist, wall chart, and so on). In the third column, list the purpose of the instructions (to give directions to visitors, to instruct students, to guide teachers, etc.). Then, in the right-hand column, evaluate each one as a good or poor example of written instructions. Be prepared to discuss your examples in class and to give one or two reasons for your evaluations.

■ Unabridged and college dictionaries include instructions explaining how to use them. In *The American Heritage Dictionary of the English Language*, Third Edition (1992), the instructions are in a section entitled "Guide to the Dictionary." *Random House Webster's College Dictionary* (1991) has a section called "Using This Dictionary," along with a sample page explaining features of the word entries. *Merriam-Webster's Collegiate Dictionary*, Tenth Edition (1993), has both an "Explanatory Chart" and "Explanatory Notes." Look into an unabridged or college dictionary and see whether its guidelines help you understand the word entries. If possible, compare dictionaries. How do the sets of instructions differ? Which one is easiest to follow? Be prepared to report your findings to your class.

Checklist of Instructions

Location	Format	Purpose	Evaluation

KEY

Location = where found

Format = book, manual, job aid, checklist, wall chart, etc.

Purpose = use and intended audience

Evaluation = good or poor example of written instructions

42

Barriers that Affect Communication: Communication Styles

A Concept Lesson with Video

Looking Ahead

What This Lesson Is About

In this lesson, you will learn about four styles of personal communication. When these styles conflict, they can cause problems in the workplace.

✔ Some people, who are called "relaters" and "socializers," pay particular attention to their relationships. Others, called "thinkers" and "directors," concentrate more on getting things done.

✔ Some people—the socializers and directors—are active and energetic. Others—the relaters and thinkers—are cautious and slow to act.

✔ If your style conflicts with the styles of your co-workers, you and they may be able to overcome this barrier by better adapting your styles to one another's.

Key Ideas

communication style—a person's customary way of relating to other persons

director—an energetic person whose emphasis is on task performance

job sharing—having the same job and work space as another person but working at different times of the day

relater—a cautious person who emphasizes relations with others

socializer—an energetic person who emphasizes relations with others

thinker—a cautious person whose emphasis is on task performance

Viewing the Videodisc—"It's Him or Me"

You are about to see the first of three videodisc or videocassette segments about Susan, a technician at a veterinary clinic. Susan shares her job with Ted—she works mornings, and he works afternoons. When co-workers share the same job—a growing trend in the workplace—they need to communicate and cooperate. Unfortunately, Susan and Ted have noticeably different communication styles.

As you watch the video segment, ask yourself,

"What is causing Susan's problems?"

"It's Him or Me"
Search 14483, Play To 18828

> *"If a person is worth knowing at all, he is worth knowing well."*
>
> —Alexander Smith, Scottish poet

Post-Viewing Questions

After you have watched the segment, answer the following questions:

1 How would you describe Susan's communication style?

2 How would you describe Ted's communication style?

3 Susan says she is going to quit. What are some of her alternatives to quitting?

Be prepared to share your answers with the class.

"It's Him or Me": Discussion Question 1
Search Frame 18829

"It's Him or Me": Discussion Question 2
Search Frame 18830

"It's Him or Me": Discussion Question 3
Search Frame 18831

Many of the clients of the Blue Sky Veterinary Clinic enjoy Ted's outgoing personality and his willingness to let them see the problem for themselves.

Getting Started

Four Communication Styles

Everyone has a distinct style of personal communication—a pattern that a person follows most of the time. Experts in the field of communication have developed various ways of classifying these styles. In *Communicating at Work*, Tony Alessandra and Phil Hunsaker identify four main styles of communication: the "relater," the "socializer," the "thinker," and the "director."

Both relaters and socializers put high priority on their interactions with other persons—they are relationship-oriented. What distinguishes the two types is that relaters are cautious, whereas socializers are energetic. Relaters tend to stay on the sidelines; socializers are more outgoing.

Both thinkers and directors put high priority on getting things done—they are task-oriented. But thinkers are cautious, whereas directors are energetic and bold, seeking to influence others.

These four personal communication styles are summarized in the diagram at right.

In your journal, answer the following questions:

1 How do you usually interact with other persons? Are you cautious or energetic? Are you relationship-oriented or task-oriented?

2 Which label best fits your communication style—

Four Styles at a Glance	
Relater • relationship-oriented • cautious • moves, acts, and speaks slowly • avoids risks • wants peace and tranquility • enjoys teamwork • has good counseling skills	**Socializer** • relationship-oriented • energetic • moves, acts, and speaks quickly • takes risks • wants excitement and change • enjoys the spotlight • has good persuasive skills
Thinker • task-oriented • cautious • moves, acts, and speaks slowly • wants to be accurate • enjoys solitary, intellectual work • makes decisions cautiously • has good problem-solving skills	**Director** • task-oriented • energetic • moves, acts, and speaks quickly • wants to be in charge • gets results through others • makes decisions quickly • has good administrative skills

Source: Tony Alessandra and Phil Hunsaker, *Communicating at Work* (New York: Fireside, Simon & Schuster, 1993), p. 44. Copyright ©1993 by Anthony J. Alessandra and Phillip L. Hunsaker. Reprinted with permission of Simon & Schuster, Inc.

relater, socializer, thinker, or director? Why do you say this? Your teacher will ask you to examine either the diagram above or the diagram on page 47 before you decide. Also, describe a recent experience that serves as an example of your style.

Adapting to Other Styles

As you saw in the video segment, conflicts may arise when persons with different styles work together. Learning to relate effectively to one another in any work setting is a process that involves all people concerned. One person can't be expected to change his or her style completely, just to accommodate another. All must strive to make whatever adjustments they can to work harmoniously together.

Because you have no control over how others will adapt their styles to yours, a good place to start is to consider how **you** might adapt your style to theirs. When you see that your style of communicating is clashing with another individual's, you might begin by identifying the other person's style. Then think about how you might make adustments in your style to adapt it to that person's. Here are some guidelines:

To work in harmony with relaters, support their need for warmth, sincerity, and trust. Express an interest in their emotions. Keep the discussion informal and relaxed.

To work in harmony with socializers, give them compliments. State your approval of their dreams and aspirations. Be a patient listener. Avoid conflict.

To work in harmony with thinkers, support their need for logical problem solving. Express an interest in their knowledge. Present information in detail. Be patient. Thinkers need time for discussion and analysis.

To work in harmony with directors, support their goals and objectives. Express an interest in their ideas. Be precise and efficient, brief and goal-oriented.

Keeping in mind the personal-style label that you chose for yourself, reread the suggestions for working in harmony with someone who has that style. Ask yourself whether these suggestions seem sensible. Do they reflect the way you would like to be treated? Why or why not? If not, are you sure you picked the right label? You may need to rethink your label.

Write a brief entry in your journal answering these questions. Also explain why you did or did not feel it was necessary to change your label.

> *"Sharing is sometimes more demanding than giving."*
>
> —Mary Catherine Bateson,
> American anthropologist and writer

Four Styles

SUPPORTING
(Relationship-oriented)

INDIRECT
(Slow Pace)

DIRECT
(Fast Pace)

CONTROLLING
(Task-oriented)

THE RELATER STYLE

- Slow at taking action and making decisions
- Likes close, personal relationships
- Dislikes interpersonal conflict
- Supports and "actively" listens to others
- Weak at goal setting and self-direction
- Has excellent ability to gain support from others
- Works slowly and cohesively with others
- Seeks security and a sense of belonging

THE SOCIALIZER STYLE

- Spontaneous actions and decisions
- Likes involvement
- Dislikes being alone
- Exaggerates and generalizes
- Tends to dream and gets others caught up in his or her dreams
- Jumps from one activity to another
- Works quickly and excitedly with others
- Seeks esteem and acknowledgment

THE THINKER STYLE

- Cautious actions and decisions
- Likes organization and structure
- Dislikes involvement
- Asks many questions about specific details
- Prefers objective, task-oriented, intellectual work environment
- Wants to be right, so can be overly reliant on data collection
- Works slowly and precisely alone

THE DIRECTOR STYLE

- Decisive actions and decisions
- Likes control, dislikes inaction
- Prefers maximum freedom to manage self and others
- Cool, independent, and competitive
- Low tolerance for feelings, attitudes, and advice of others
- Works quickly and impressively alone

Source: Tony Alessandra and Phil Hunsaker, *Communicating at Work* (New York: Fireside, Simon & Schuster, 1993), p. 32. Copyright ©1993 by Anthony J. Alessandra and Phillip L. Hunsaker. Reprinted with permission of Simon & Schuster, Inc.

Trying It Out

Viewing the Videodisc—"This Has to Stop"

The first video segment showed a clash between Susan's and Ted's styles of communication. In the next segment, their boss, Dr. Gloria Romero, tries to help them.

As you watch the segment, ask yourself,

> "How can Susan and Ted work together to solve their problems?"

Post-Viewing Questions

After you have watched the video segment, answer the following questions. Use what you learned in **Getting Started** to help you do your analysis.

1 Do you agree with the doctor's description of Susan's and Ted's communication styles? Why or why not?

2 What are some things that Susan can do to adapt to Ted's communication style?

3 What are some things that Ted can do to adapt to Susan's communication style?

Be prepared to share your answers with the class.

"This Has to Stop"

Search 18839, Play To 20502

"This Has to Stop":
Discussion Question 1

Search Frame 20503

"This Has to Stop":
Discussion Question 2

Search Frame 20504

"This Has to Stop":
Discussion Question 3

Search Frame 20505

> *Ted: "I'm trying to adjust to Susan's style. But we're as different as cats and dogs."*

The "relater" and the "director" have different approaches to customer service.

Summing Up

Viewing the Videodisc—"It's Getting Better"

You are about to see the final video segment of the story, in which Susan and Ted try to adapt to each other's communication style.

As you watch the segment, ask yourself,

"How well do Susan and Ted adapt to each other's style?"

"It's Getting Better"

Search 20513, Play To 22281

In a meeting after working hours, Dr. Romero reassures Susan by telling her that she couldn't run the clinic without Susan's terrific ability to organize and complete detailed work. She also compliments Ted on his willingness to try new ideas.

Post-Viewing Questions

After you have watched the segment, answer the following questions:

1 What did Ted do to adapt to Susan's communication style?

2 What did Susan do to adapt to Ted's communication style?

3 What more could they do to improve communication between them? Use what you learned in **Getting Started** to help you answer this question.

Be prepared to share your answers with the class.

"It's Getting Better":
Discussion Question 1

Search Frame 22282

"It's Getting Better":
Discussion Question 2

Search Frame 22283

"It's Getting Better":
Discussion Question 3

Search Frame 22284

Keeping Track

On a separate piece of paper, answer the following questions. Use what you learned in this lesson to help you.

1 What are the four basic styles of personal communication?

2 How do these different personal styles create communication barriers in the workplace?

3 How can you overcome communication-style conflicts with co-workers?

Going Further

■ Think of a friend outside of class or a relative at home whose personal communication style sometimes clashes with your own. Without telling the other person, try adapting your style to fit better with his or hers. First decide which label fits the other person's style. Then follow the guidelines given in **Getting Started** for adjusting your style to another person's. After trying the experiment for several days, write a brief entry in your journal describing your experience.

■ Learn more about job sharing in today's workplace. Look up articles and books on job sharing in the school or public library. Find out why job sharing is more popular now than ever before. What are the advantages of job sharing for employers? What are the advantages for employees? How does job sharing work in various kinds of businesses and industries? What kinds of problems arise among workers who job-share? How do companies and employees resolve conflicts among job sharers? Take notes as you do your research, then write a few paragraphs reporting what you discover. Be prepared to share your findings with the class and with your instructor.

Challenging Language Traps

A Strategies Lesson

Looking Ahead

What This Lesson Is About

In this lesson, you will learn how to deal with a special kind of communication barrier in the workplace—language traps.

✔ People set up language traps when they use hurtful words or phrases about other persons or groups.

✔ You can challenge language traps in the workplace with direct and assertive communication.

✔ The DESC strategy—**D**escribe, **E**xpress, **S**pecify, **C**onsequences—can help you challenge a language trap without causing an angry confrontation.

One way to avoid language traps is to approach people as individuals who want to be appreciated for what they are, not stereotyped by how they look.

51

Spotting a Language Trap

All of us have been called names—and it hurts. But have you ever heard someone use language that hurt some other person? Did you ignore what you heard, or did you challenge the words that were used? What happened?

Write a short passage in your journal that describes the experience.

Getting Started

Language Traps

Anyone can be the victim of a language trap. We all have characteristics that someone else can belittle or bad-mouth, whether intentionally or not.

Language traps come in all shapes and sizes. They may be racist or sexist remarks. They may be negative comments about a person's appearance, gender, physical or mental abilities, age, or some other characteristic.

In the workplace, where persons of many types and persuasions come together to earn a living, such language traps may create conflicts that keep tasks from being accomplished. Their use also creates an unhealthy, dehumanizing, and disempowering environment within an organization. For these reasons, it is useful to learn how to spot language traps and how to challenge them. You should learn to recognize at least four kinds of language traps:

- **Dehumanization**: treating people as cases or problems instead of as persons

- **Over-generalization or stereotyping**: speaking of a large group of people as if they all share the characteristics of a few

- **Categorizing**: treating people as if they are defined by only one of their activities or roles

- **Polarization**: suggesting that other people are somehow different from and inferior to oneself

> "We all know we are unique individuals, but we tend to see others as representatives of groups."
>
> —Deborah Tannen, American sociolinguist and writer

Challenging the Traps

If you find yourself the victim of one of these language traps, or if you observe one of the traps as an interested bystander, you can challenge the unfair words and attitudes by using the DESC strategy. As noted earlier, these four letters stand for Describe, Express, Specify, and Consequences. Here are the steps in the process:

1 To the person who set up the language trap, **describe** which words or actions disturb and offend you. Be assertive. Also be brief, specific, and truthful. State exactly which words or actions you consider objectionable.

Don't say: "You're always calling me names."

Do say: "In speaking to me (or other women), you sometimes use words like 'gal,' 'dear,' and 'honey' in a way I do not like."

2 **Express** how the other person's words or actions make you feel. Again, be specific.

Don't say: "You're sexist."

Do say: "I believe that these terms are inappropriate."

3 **Specify** how you want the other person to change. Be reasonable. Don't ask for too much change all at once. A commitment to change is good enough to start. Avoid using words such as "should" and "ought."

Don't say: "You should keep your mouth shut from now on."

Do say: "I hope you will not use those words when you're speaking to me (or anyone else)."

4 State the possible **consequences**. Good things will happen if the other person changes; therefore, always describe these desirable outcomes. On the other hand, bad things might happen if the other person does not change—describe these bad outcomes if you must, but try to avoid making a threat. That should be a last resort. Never promise a negative consequence unless it is a reasonable response to the offense and you are willing to carry it out in an ethical manner.

Don't say: "If you call me that one more time, I'll never speak to you again!"

Do say: "When I don't hear you using these names, I feel that our working relationship will improve a lot."

> *"What is repugnant to every human being is to be reckoned always as a member of a class and not as an individual person."*
>
> —Dorothy L. Sayers, English mystery writer and essayist

The DESC Technique was developed by Sharon Anthony Bower and Gordon H. Bower and explained in Chapter 5 of *Asserting Yourself: A Practical Guide for Positive Change,* Updated Edition, ©1991 by Sharon Anthony Bower and Gordon H. Bower. This material is adapted and reprinted by permission of Addison-Wesley Publishing Company, Inc., and the authors.

In using the DESC strategy, it is always appropriate to be assertive. Being assertive means that you state your case clearly, firmly, and truthfully. Being assertive is **not**

- ridiculing or blaming your antagonist.

- exaggerating your complaints.

- stooping to use the same kinds of labels, stereotypes, or unfair generalizations that your antagonist uses.

- turning a minor problem into a major confrontation.

- lecturing, preaching, or telling someone what kind of person he or she should be.

Each of these communication behaviors is **aggressive**, not assertive.

Trying It Out

The Manager's Complaint

As you read the following story, ask yourself what kinds of language traps appear, and think about how Gladys could use the DESC strategy to respond to the behavior that troubles her.

Gladys is working in the kitchen of a fast-food restaurant. Her boss is flipping hamburgers at the grill. He starts in on his nightly ritual—making angry remarks but never doing anything about the situation that's upsetting him.

"We have to figure out some way to handle those retards that come in here from that group home up the road," he tells Gladys. "They're all goofy. Customers don't like to see them in here." Wiping his hands on his apron, he adds, "We're not running a loony bin. We have a right not to serve weirdos if they cause problems."

Gladys finds his remarks offensive. She has a younger sister who has Down's syndrome. And anyway, some of the customers from the group home may talk a little loudly, but they never cause any real trouble in the restaurant.

Use the DESC strategy to formulate a response that Gladys could make to change her boss's behavior. Be sure to include each component of DESC: Describe, Express, Specify, and Consequences. On a separate piece of paper, finish the story by describing what Gladys says to her boss and how her boss reacts.

Be prepared to share your story with the class.

54

Finding a Career in the Kitchen

Do you love to cook or bake? Do you enjoy working with food and serving people? If you do, you might consider a job in the food industry. Food-industry jobs cover everything from kitchen aides to food photographers, space-food scientists, and restaurant owners. Today more than 7.5 million people work in food preparation and service—a total that should rise by 25 percent to 33 percent in the next 10 years.

Although many people in this industry learn on the job, you can increase your chance of advancement with training in the culinary arts. Students in the many one- or two-year programs in the United States can continue to work as they improve their job prospects. Graduating chefs from the Culinary Institute of America in Hyde Park, New York, can expect several job offers and starting salaries of about $23,000.

And if you thought of work in a fast-food restaurant as an after-school job with little career potential, think again. According to a University of California study of 2,000 young men who did not attend college, one in four of those who took restaurant jobs reached a managerial position within four years.

So if you enjoy working with food, consider turning your interest into a full-time career in the fast-growing food industry.

—Adapted from "Want a Job in Food?"
Parade magazine (Nov. 13, 1994).

> *"The fact that we are human beings is infinitely more important than all the peculiarities that distinguish human beings from one another."*
>
> —Simone de Beauvoir,
> French writer, philosopher

Summing Up

DESC at Work

The DESC strategy gives you a way to negotiate positive relationships with supervisors, co-workers, and others. But could you really use it in the workplace?

Work with a partner to create your own brief role-playing skit for a real-life situation involving a language trap in the workplace.

55

Choose one of the four types of language traps to demonstrate in your act. Then have one partner set the trap and the other partner challenge it by using the DESC strategy. Plan your words carefully, following the guidelines in **Getting Started**.

Be prepared to perform your act for the class and to comment on how well your classmates used the DESC procedure in their performances.

Keeping Track

On a separate piece of paper, answer the following questions. Use what you have learned in this lesson to help you.

1 What are four kinds of language traps?

2 What are the four steps in the DESC strategy for challenging language traps?

3 What does "assertive" mean as it relates to using the DESC strategy?

> *"It is almost impossible to throw dirt on someone without getting a little on yourself."*
> —Abigail Van Buren, American advice columnist

Going Further

■ Practice using the DESC strategy with a friend outside class. Follow the four DESC steps. Be assertive and specific—but don't forget to be reasonable and positive at the same time. Then assess the outcome. What happened? Did your use of the strategy have a good effect? If not, what went wrong? Be prepared to share your experience with the class and your teacher.

■ Low humor has traditionally relied on language traps for its effect. There are jokes about every group imaginable. Situation comedies (sitcoms) on TV have built their shows around the use of such language. During the next several days, as you watch television or movies, listen carefully for language traps. On a separate piece of paper, list the traps you hear. Be prepared to share your findings with your class and with your teacher.

Persuasive Communication

A Literature Lesson

Looking Ahead

What This Lesson Is About

In this lesson, you will read a short speech entitled "I Have a Dream," which was delivered by Dr. Martin Luther King, Jr., at the March on Washington on August 28, 1963. It is probably the best-known and most influential oral presentation of the second half of the 20th century in the United States.

☑ One of the best ways to learn how to speak persuasively is to listen to people who express themselves effectively and who capture their audiences—people such as Dr. King. Such skills can be used in a variety of situations, not just in public speaking.

☑ Persuasive communication is not so easy as it looks. It involves knowing the audience and using examples they understand. It involves careful attention not only to **what** you say but also to **how** you say it: the words you choose, your tone of voice, and the gestures you use.

☑ But no communication can fully persuade unless, as Dr. King's address does, it carries a message that speaks to the feelings and needs of the people who are listening to it.

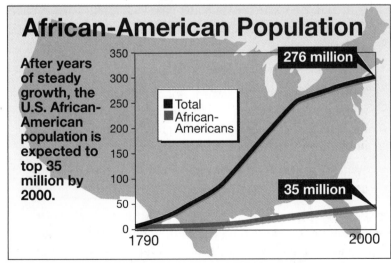

African-American Population

After years of steady growth, the U.S. African-American population is expected to top 35 million by 2000.

276 million

35 million

■ Total
■ African-Americans

350
300
250
200
150
100
50
0

1790   2000

Source: U.S. Census Bureau

"Telling It Like It Is"

Have you ever listened to a speaker who held you spellbound? Perhaps one of your teachers (or a family member, a preacher, a political figure, or a television personality) could really capture and hold your attention.

In your journal, write about this speaker. Try to explain what made the person's speech so powerful. Was it good word choice, effective delivery style, beautiful voice, great ideas—or all of the above? Be prepared to share your work with the class.

Getting Started

"I Have a Dream" by Dr. Martin Luther King, Jr.

The 1963 March on Washington, which sought guarantees of civil rights for blacks and all other Americans, was the largest gathering ever assembled up to that time in the nation's capital. Lerone Bennett, Jr., who was there, described the day's high point, which occurred at the Lincoln Memorial 100 years after the signing of the Emancipation Proclamation:

> "A second man, now: Martin Luther King, Jr., coming to the lectern late in the afternoon, when the shadows were long on the grass. He read for a time from a prepared speech and then he began to improvise, speaking of a dream big enough to include all men and all children, speaking of the day when little black boys and little black girls would join hands with little white boys and little white girls as brothers and sisters.

> "'I have a dream,' he said, over and over, and each elaboration evoked hysterical cheers.

> "It was not so much the words, eloquent as they were, as the manner of saying them....The rhythms and intonation called back all the struggle and all the pain and all the agony, and held forth the possibility of triumph....

> "When King finished, grown men and women wept unashamedly."

As you read "I Have a Dream," pay close attention to how Dr. King's point comes across on the printed page. Try to imagine—or perhaps you have seen a film of the event—how his voice must have sounded and what emotions he expressed.

I Have a Dream

I say to you today, my friends, even though we face the difficulties of today and tomorrow, I still have a dream. It is a dream deeply rooted in the American dream. I have a dream that one day this nation will rise up and live out the true meaning of its creed, "We hold these truths to be self-evident; that all men are created equal." I have a dream that one day on the red hills of Georgia, sons of former slaves and the sons of former slave owners will be able to sit down together at the table of brotherhood. I have a dream that one day even the state of Mississippi, a state sweltering with the heat of injustice, sweltering with the heat of oppression, will be transformed into an oasis of freedom and justice. I have a dream

American dream—a phrase coined in 1933 that refers to an American social ideal that stresses egalitarianism (equal opportunity) and especially material prosperity

oppression—unjust or cruel use of power over others

Selected portions from the "I Have a Dream" speech, addressing the March on Washington, D.C., August 28, 1963. Reprinted by arrangement with The Heirs to the Estate of Martin Luther King, Jr., c/o Joan Daves Agency, as agent for the proprietor. ©1963 by Martin Luther King, Jr.; copyright renewed 1991 by Coretta Scott King.

Provided by and used by permission of Archive Photos.

In 1963 more than 200,000 people gathered at the Lincoln Memorial in Washington, D.C., and stood for more than three hours listening to speakers who demanded the passage of the Civil Rights Bill. The speakers included Mahalia Jackson, John Lewis, and Martin Luther King., Jr., who delivered his famous "I Have a Dream" speech.

59

interposition—the disputed doctrine that a state may reject a federal order that it regards as intruding on the state's rights

nullification—the refusal of a state to enforce a federal law

hew—to cut something out of something else and give it a new shape (for example, "They hewed the farms out of the wilderness.")

prodigious—extraordinary in bulk or degree; enormous

hamlet—a small village

that my four little children will one day live in a nation where they will not be judged by the color of their skin, but by the content of their character.

I have a dream today!

I have a dream that one day down in Alabama—with its vicious racists, with its Governor having his lips dripping with the words of interposition and nullification—one day right there in Alabama, little black boys and black girls will be able to join hands with little white boys and white girls as sisters and brothers.

I have a dream today!

I have a dream that one day every valley shall be exalted, and every hill and mountain shall be made low. The rough places will be plain and the crooked places will be made straight, "and the glory of the Lord shall be revealed, and all flesh shall see it together."

This is our hope. This is the faith that I go back to the South with. With this faith we will be able to hew out of the mountain of despair a stone of hope. With this faith we will be able to transform the jangling discords of our nation into a beautiful symphony of brotherhood. With this faith we will be able to work together, to pray together, to struggle together, to go to jail together, to stand up for freedom together, knowing that we will be free one day. And this will be the day. This will be the day when all of God's children will be able to sing with new meaning, "My country 'tis of thee, sweet land of liberty, of thee I sing. Land where my fathers died, land of the pilgrims' pride, from every mountainside, let freedom ring." And if America is to be a great nation, this must become true.

So let freedom ring from the prodigious hilltops of New Hampshire; let freedom ring from the mighty mountains of New York; let freedom ring from the heightening Alleghenies of Pennsylvania; let freedom ring from the snow-capped Rockies of Colorado; let freedom ring from the curvaceous slopes of California. But not only that. Let freedom ring from Stone Mountain of Georgia; let freedom ring from Lookout Mountain of Tennessee; let freedom ring from every hill and molehill of Mississippi. "From every mountainside, let freedom ring."

And when this happens, and when we allow freedom to ring, when we let it ring from every village and every hamlet, from every state and every city, we will be able to speed up that day when all of God's children—black men and white men, Jews and Gentiles, Protestants and Catholics—will be able to join hands and sing in the words of the old Negro spiritual, "Free at last. Free at last. Thank God Almighty, we are free at last."

60

Meet Martin Luther King, Jr.

The powerful speeches of Martin Luther King, Jr., expressed black Americans' yearning for justice during the 1950s and '60s, when segregation was the law in the South. As the leader of the civil rights movement, King organized nonviolent demonstrations to change the law, supported by millions of people of all races. His efforts bore fruit when Congress passed the Civil Rights Act of 1964, which banned racial discrimination in public places. He received the Nobel Peace Prize that same year.

A Baptist minister, King based his nonviolent philosophy on the principles of Christianity; however, his opponents often used violence against him. In Chicago he was the target of stone-throwing mobs, and his home in Montgomery, Alabama, was bombed. Then in 1968 he was shot to death in Memphis, Tennessee.

His assassination saddened and angered many people. Riots broke out in more than 100 cities. Within a few months, Congress passed the Civil Rights Act of 1968, prohibiting discrimination in most housing. Years later his birthday was declared a national holiday, making him only the second American to receive this honor—the first was George Washington.

King was born in 1929 in Atlanta, Georgia. He did so well in high school that he skipped the ninth and 12th grades, and he entered Morehouse College when he was only 15. He was the author of five books: *Stride Toward Freedom*, *Strength to Love*, *Why We Can't Wait*, *Where Do We Go from Here: Chaos or Community?*, and *The Trumpet of Conscience*.

Civil Rights Act

The Civil Rights Act of 1964 is one of the United States' strongest civil rights laws. The act bans discrimination based on a person's color, race, national origin, religion, or sex. Rights covered by the act include the right—guaranteed to everyone—to seek employment, to vote, and to use hotels, parks, restaurants, and other public places.

Trying It Out

. . . .

Responding to "I Have a Dream"

How did the speech make you feel? Write a sentence or two in your journal describing your reaction to the speech.

Now listen as Dr. King's speech is delivered orally.

After hearing the speech, write another sentence or two describing your reactions to the oral presentation. Note any differences between your reactions when you read the speech and when you heard it delivered.

61

Dissecting the Speech

The reactions you recorded in your journal are very significant. The ultimate goal of any speaker is to have an impact on the audience. If you were "caught up" in the speech, if you felt moved by it, if you were inspired to share Dr. King's dream and to work to make it a reality, he accomplished his purpose.

But if you want to learn how to construct and deliver an effective persuasive speech, it is helpful to look closely at a good example, such as this one, and see **why** it is effective and **how** the speaker reaches the audience.

Dr. King used several strategies that are common to speeches intended to persuade or convince. These strategies are:

- **Establish a common bond with the audience.** Use examples and language that will convince your listeners that you are "one of them," that you share a common concern.

- **Focus on one or two key ideas.** Introducing too many ideas or issues will confuse the audience and leave them with no clear idea of what you have said. Keep it simple.

- **Support your ideas with references to respected authorities.** Use quotations from well-known sources that are familiar and accepted by your audience to reinforce what you say.

- **Describe clearly how the audience will benefit from your recommendation.** Avoid generalities by painting a clear, visual picture of the potential benefits.

- **Help your audience understand and remember what you are saying.** Use short sentences and repetition to keep your audience on track, to hold their attention, and to help them retain your message. Understand that people comprehend spoken and written language differently.

Reread the speech as you complete your copy of the **Tools for Persuasive Speaking** form. After reading each sentence of "I Have a Dream," ask yourself whether it reflects one of the persuasive strategies. When you have completed your form, compare answers with your classmates. Did you miss anything?

> "What Martin Luther King understood, and used with great effectiveness, was the fact that blacks and whites alike ultimately shared a common moral universe in this country. However much racism there might be, this moral universe not only limited how far it could go, this common set of moral values even galvanized into action whites who did not necessarily share the goals of the civil rights movement."
>
> —Thomas Sowell, "Civil Rights Leadership at the Crossroads," Creators Syndicate

Tools for Persuasive Speaking

Strategy	Examples from "I Have a Dream"
Bond with audience.	
Focus on one or two ideas.	
Cite authorities.	
Show benefits.	
Repeat key ideas.	

Summing Up

A Spellbinder

Now that you know about the strategies for creating a persuasive speech, look back at the journal entry you wrote at the beginning of this lesson. Analyze the approach of the speaker you described. How did he or she bond with the audience? What was the focus of the speech? What benefits were promised? What authorities were quoted? Did the speaker use repetition or a recurring phrase that sticks in your mind?

Rewrite your description, basing your evaluation of the speaker on these five persuasive strategies.

Be prepared to share your work with the class.

On Power, Justice, and History

Power at its best is love implementing the demands of justice. Justice at its best is love correcting everything that stands against love.

Darkness cannot drive out darkness; only light can do that. Hate cannot drive out hate; only love can do that. Hate multiplies hate, violence multiplies violence, and toughness multiplies toughness in a descending spiral of destruction....The chain reaction of evil—hate begetting hate, wars producing more wars—must be broken, or we shall be plunged into the dark abyss of annihilation.

If you will protest courageously, and yet with dignity and Christian love, when the history books are written in future generations, the historians will have to pause and say, "There lived a great people—a black people—who injected new meaning and dignity into the veins of civilization."

—Martin Luther King, Jr.

Keeping Track

On a separate piece of paper, answer the following questions. Use what you have learned in this lesson to help you with your answers.

1 Why is it important to listen to or read the speeches of skilled communicators?

2 What strategies do effective speakers use to persuade their audiences?

3 What are two powerful ingredients in Dr. King's speech that can help every communicator?

Going Further

■ Dr. King's speech was very brief—only 617 words. Another very brief speech that has become a classic is President Abraham Lincoln's "Gettysburg Address." Find a copy of Lincoln's address in your library, and read it carefully, comparing it in tone, word choice, and message to Dr. King's speech. Then examine it to determine which of the five strategies Lincoln used. Read the speech aloud, imagining how it sounded to the audience. If your library has a recording of a dramatic reading of the speech, listen to that too. Summarize your comparison of the two speeches in a form that you find appropriate—either in a brief paper or as a chart. Be prepared to share your work with the class and to turn it in to your teacher.

■ As you may have gathered from Lerone Bennett's description of the 1963 March on Washington, the experience left a deep impression on everyone who participated. To understand its impact and the powerful effect of Dr. King's speech, read a book or some magazine articles about the civil rights movement. Find out what the issues were and what it was like to participate in huge demonstrations and to register voters in the South. If possible, find someone in your community who took part in the 1963 march and interview him or her for a firsthand account. Then summarize what you learn in a two-page paper. Be prepared to share it with the class and to turn it in to your teacher.

■ Senator Robert F. Kennedy, who served as U.S. Attorney General and was a candidate for president, was assassinated in 1968, the same year that Dr. King was killed. Kennedy also spoke of dreams. He said, "Some men see things as they are and say, 'Why?' I dream things that never were and say, 'Why not?'" More than a quarter of a century later, what is the state of the American dream today—of the King and Kennedy dreams for social equality? Do their dreams live on? Have they been fulfilled, or do they need to be revived? Are you a person who asks "Why?" or "Why not?" Write a persuasive essay (or speech, if you prefer) to convince your readers or listeners that (a) the dream has been fulfilled or (b) we need to rekindle the dream and ask "Why not?"

■ Watch several minutes of television newscasts each day for a week, noting persons who are persuasive speakers delivering important messages. Jot down notes on how they get their points across. List their main points, along with the words or phrases they use to explain them. Also note your own responses to their messages. How do these speakers make you feel? Write a brief report on one especially effective example. Be prepared to share what you write with the class.

> *"Oppressed people cannot remain oppressed forever. The urge for freedom will eventually come. This is what has happened to the American Negro. Something within has reminded him of his birthright of freedom; something without has reminded him that he can gain it...."*
>
> —Martin Luther King, Jr., Letter from Birmingham City Jail

65

The Springarn Medal

The Springarn Medal was instituted in 1914 by the late J.E. Springarn, then chairman of the board of directors of the National Association for the Advancement of Colored People (NAACP). The medal, which is awarded annually, "recognizes the highest or noblest achievement by an American Negro." In July 1994, Maya Angelou became the 79th Springarn Medalist. Several previous honorees are listed below.

William Edward Burghardt (W.E.B.) DuBois
George Washington Carver
Marian Anderson
Charles Drew
Paul Robeson
Thurgood Marshall
Ralph J. Bunche
Mabel Keaton Staupers
Jack Roosevelt (Jackie) Robinson
Martin Luther King, Jr.
Mrs. Daisy Bates and the Little Rock Nine
Edward Kennedy (Duke) Ellington
Langston Hughes
Medgar Wiley Evers
Roy Wilkins
Leontyne Price

Edward W. Brooke
Sammy Davis, Jr.
Henry (Hank) Aaron
Alvin Ailey
Alex Haley
Andrew Young
Rosa L. Parks
Coleman Young
Lena Horne
Thomas Bradley
Bill Cosby
Dr. Benjamin L. Hooks
Frederick Douglass Patterson
Jesse Jackson
L. Douglas Wilder
General Colin L. Powell
Barbara Jordan
Dorothy Height

"Out of the huts of history's shame I rise—bringing the gifts that my ancestors gave, I am the dream and the hope of the slave. I rise I rise I rise."

—Maya Angelou

Presenting Your Point of View in Oral Presentations

A Concept Lesson

Looking Ahead

What This Lesson Is About

In this lesson, you will learn how to plan, prepare, and deliver persuasive oral presentations.

☑ Oral presentations are messages spoken to one person, several persons, or many persons.

☑ You can use a regular procedure to develop persuasive oral presentations.

☑ It is empowering to be able to speak effectively to your supervisors and co-workers in various workplace situations.

Telling a new co-worker how to complete a task is one example of an informal oral presentation.

Tongue Untied

In the workplace, many occasions arise to deliver spoken messages. You may need to tell a new co-worker about workplace rules. You may need to instruct a co-worker on using a new computer. Or you may need to persuade co-workers at a staff meeting to see things your way.

For some people, spoken interaction of any kind does not come easily. Consider the following story:

> Tyrone has been working for three years as a mechanic's assistant at an automobile repair shop near his home. He loves the work and has learned a great deal about the shop's specialty, Mercedes products. But Tyrone has always been shy and somewhat tongue-tied. He prefers to listen as his boss and his fellow workers do the talking rather than to speak up himself.
>
> Yesterday the boss told Tyrone that he is the best assistant mechanic the garage has and that he is planning to promote him to the position of mechanic as soon as a slot becomes vacant. Tyrone was happy at first—the promotion would mean more pay and better hours—but then he realized that it also meant he would be responsible for telling the assistants what to do and how to do it. That prospect frightens him, and he is thinking about telling his boss he would rather remain an assistant.

Put yourself in Tyrone's place. On a separate piece of paper, answer the following questions:

■ Why does the thought of having to give instructions to the other assistants frighten you? Are you unsure of your mechanical knowledge—or of your ability to communicate? If you decide to take the promotion, what could you do to overcome your fear of making oral presentations? If you decide to turn down the promotion, what effect will that have on your future with the company and your relationship with the boss?

> *"It's been said that communicating is 10% words, 30% sounds, and 60% body language. I listen with my eyes."*
>
> —Heather Carson, lighting director; quoted in *Lighting Dimensions* (November 1994)

Be prepared to share your answers with the class.

Getting Started

Making a Speech

In Lesson 9, you read Dr. Martin Luther King's "I Have a Dream" speech, which was delivered to a crowd of a quarter million people. Do you think he was nervous at the prospect of standing up in front of such a large audience, with millions of others watching on television? As a minister, he was a seasoned speaker—but this was something more than addressing his own congregation.

Although we don't know how he really felt at that moment, we can assume that whatever nervousness he might have felt was reduced because:

- He knew his audience. These were people who believed in equality and freedom.

- He knew what he wanted to say. Even though, as Lerone Bennett reports, he did not use his prepared speech, he knew the subject well and had spoken many times before on the same issue.

- He believed in the message he was delivering.

So what does that have to do with how **you** approach the task of communicating orally—either to a few people or to a large audience? You may not have Dr. King's experience or gift for oratory, but you can bolster your confidence and do a good job by taking the time to:

"Where shall I begin, please your majesty?" she asked.

"Begin at the beginning," the king said, very gravely, *"and go on till you come to the end: then stop."*

—Lewis Carroll, pseudonym (pen name) of Charles Dodgson, *Alice's Adventures in Wonderland*

1 Know your audience.

2 Research your subject.

3 Build a logical argument to convince your audience.

4 Plan what you are going to say.

5 Rehearse and revise what you are going to say.

6 Say it!

Now let's see how this process works on the job.

Assume that, as the senior employee in the assembly division of an electronics firm, you have been asked to make a two- to three-minute presentation about the new safety regulations. This is not to be simply an informative talk explaining the regulations. That's already been done.

The problem is that nobody is paying attention to the regulations. Your job is to convince the people in your department to use safety glasses, to turn off the power whenever they are assembling an item, and to use the new insulated hand tools instead of the old ones with metal handles.

69

The American poet and essayist Ralph Waldo Emerson once said that "Speech is power: speech is to persuade, to convert, to compel."

Good preparation will help you tap into that power.

In preparing for your presentation, you follow the six-step process outlined on the previous page:

1 Know your audience.

You already know the audience since they're your co-workers, but do you know why they are resisting the regulations? You need to talk informally with them to find out what their objections are.

You learn that most of the workers object to wearing safety glasses because the goggles look weird. They don't always turn the power off because they have to keep testing the equipment, and it's too much trouble (or they forget) to turn it off every time a screw needs tightening. And the old tools work better because they've been "broken in."

2 Research the subject.

If the reasons for using the new procedures weren't covered in the information session, you may need to talk with your supervisor or the person in charge of carrying out the regulations. It wouldn't hurt to do some library research on industrial accidents, especially eye injuries and electrical accidents. Look for authorities you can quote—or get a good quote from the president of the company expressing his concern for the workers' safety.

You find out that 10,000 workers die every year from workplace accidents and that another 15,000 are seriously injured. The majority of the accidents are the result of failing to follow safety precautions. Electrical accidents are the leading cause of injuries in your industry, followed closely by serious eye injuries caused by flying particles. The president of the company, in his introduction to the employee manual, has stated, "We want to be a profitable company, but our employees' safety is our first priority."

3 Build a convincing argument.

To be convincing, your argument must be logical; in other words, it must make sense to the audience and build a case that they should do what you want them to do. This is also the place to anticipate workers' objections and to deal with those issues before your listeners have a chance to voice them and put you on the defensive.

You decide that you will base your case on three facts: (1) It's better to see well than to look good; moreover, because eye injuries can blind you, it's much better to use the glasses; (2) It takes two seconds to flip the power switch; do it regularly and it will become a habit that can save your life; (3) It won't take long to "break in" the new tools—but you'll never get used to them if you don't use them.

4 **Plan the talk.**

Here's where you need to refer to the strategies you learned in Lesson 9:

• **Establish a common bond with the audience.**

You decide to point out that you're all members of a team. You understand how other workers feel because you don't like the safety glasses either and you have trouble remembering to turn off the power. But you want to share what you've learned about accidents.

• **Focus on a limited number of ideas.**

Your one central message is, "Follow the new regulations." The three sub-points are "wear the glasses"; "remember to turn off the power"; and "use the insulated tools."

• **Refer to authorities.**

Your authorities are the statistics that you gathered and the president's statement that worker safety is the company's top priority.

• **Show the benefits of doing what you say.**

The benefits are avoiding serious injury, possibly even death; maintaining a good safety record for the department; and impressing the bosses by cooperating.

• **Help your audience remember what you are saying.**

In your conclusion, you decide to appeal to their concern for their own safety and their spirit of cooperation as a team.

5 **Rehearse and revise.**

It's important to know how your talk will "go over." Find some friends who will be an audience for your rehearsal—but don't use members of the work group that you will be addressing. Consider your friends' suggestions, and revise your plan where you think it should be changed.

6 **Give your presentation.**

You will do this later in the lesson.

In an "informative presentation" (for example, the simple explanation of the new safety regulations that was originally given to your co-workers), the speaker relays information objectively, with no particular effort to convince the audience to agree or to act in a specific way. But in a "persuasive presentation" (for instance, the assignment you are doing in this lesson), the speaker must organize the information to build a case, much as a lawyer in a courtroom does. A persuasive speaker has to use information

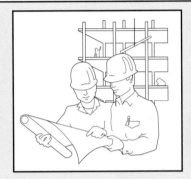

"Ten thousand Americans die every year from occupational injuries—almost 40 each working day. Up to 100,000 more die from occupational disease—almost 400 each working day. Every five seconds, a worker is injured on the job."

—Edward M. Kennedy,
United States senator
from Massachusetts

71

to support a particular point of view and to convince the audience to agree or to take action.

■ Look back at the six steps and the strategies you have just read. Which of these pertain specifically to persuasive speaking? Which are appropriate for any oral presentation?

■ Why is it especially important to know your audience when you are planning a persuasive talk?

■ Why is it helpful to use data or quotations from authorities when doing a persuasive presentation?

Trying It Out

Preparing, Rehearsing, and Presenting

Using the information you received in the previous section, create and be prepared to deliver a three- to five-minute persuasive oral presentation to the group of co-workers.

Preparing

Outline what you plan to say. This outline should include three sections:

1 the **introduction**, in which you establish your common bond with the members of your audience and get their attention for what you are planning to say. You can gain attention by using a bold and surprising statement, a personal story, or a striking visual aid—a picture of someone in a hospital bed or a graph showing the number of workplace accidents. Introductions to informative oral presentations don't need to be so dramatic, but a bit of showmanship can't hurt when you are trying to persuade.

2 the **body**, in which you convey your main message. What is the problem? What are the risks of not doing what you recommend? What are the benefits of following your recommendation? What do experts (in this case, the company president) say about the problem?

3 the **conclusion**, in which you summarize what you have said and challenge your audience to take action.

Outlining allows you to experiment with various arrangements of your information and ideas. It can also be a useful tool when the time comes to deliver your oral presentation. Delivering your talk from an outline rather than from a written speech often makes for a fresh, spontaneous speaking style. It also encourages you to maintain eye contact with your listeners.

When you have completed your outline, review it to see whether you need any visual aids—posters, handouts, or overhead transparencies. If pictures or graphs would help you get your message across, prepare them and decide where they would best fit into your presentation.

Rehearsing

Are you nervous about speaking in front of a group? Even such noted speakers as Winston Churchill and Mahatma Gandhi have admitted to becoming speechless the first few times they faced an audience.

Fortunately there are ways to control the "butterflies" in your stomach. You have already done some important things: You've decided what to say, and you've planned how you will say it. To increase your confidence, try out your presentation on a small audience of friends or classmates. Then make any changes that you think will improve it.

Another good way to control your nervousness is to exercise both your lungs and your body. Take slow, deep breaths. This has a physiological effect on your body, telling it, "Hey, this is no emergency. Slow down." Move around too. Exercise burns up the excess adrenaline in your body. Before the presentation, take a walk, or do aerobics or some other kind of exercise. While you're waiting to speak, deliberately tense and relax your legs, hands, and arms. No one will notice this except you—and you'll feel calmer.

Keeping Your Eyes on Your Audience

Maintaining eye contact with your audience is important for several reasons.

1. Frequent and steady eye contact will give your audience the impression that you believe in your message. By showing your willingness to "look them in the eye," you will increase the audience's interest in what you have to say.

2. You will gain valuable feedback as you look among members of your audience, turning your gaze to include all of a small group or as many sections of a large group as you can. If some people look bored, you may want to speak with more energy or cover the material more quickly. If some look confused, you may want to re-state your last point in a different way to help them understand.

3. Maintaining frequent eye contact sends a nonverbal message to your audience that you know your material so well that a few casual glances at your outline are all you need to make your presentation.

The surest way to give yourself the confidence to keep your eyes on your audience is to keep your eyes on your material **before** the presentation—in other words, prepare and practice until you can cover the material without hesitation.

Presenting

Deliver your talk before the class. Imagine that your classmates are the co-workers who have not been following the new safety regulations. Present your talk as a group, with one person giving the introduction, another person the body, and a third person the conclusion. One of you (or a fourth member of your group) can be in charge of visual aids, if you use any.

The "co-workers" will ask questions and make comments. Be prepared to respond. They will also use copies of the **Oral Presentation Rating Sheet** to evaluate your group's presentation; you will do the same for them when they give their presentations.

Be prepared to discuss the feedback you receive with the class.

Oral Presentation Rating Sheet

Presenter _____   Evaluator _____

Aspect of Presentation	Excellent	Good	Fair	Poor
INTRODUCTION				
Did the presenter establish a bond with me?				
Did the presenter grab my attention?				
Did the presenter preview the topic?				
BODY				
Did the presenter give relevant data?				
Did the presenter build a logical argument?				
Were the visual aids appropriate?				
Were authorities quoted?				
CONCLUSION				
Did the presenter summarize key points?				
Was there a call to action?				
GENERAL				
Was the presenter convincing?				
Did the presenter speak clearly?				
Did the presenter appear relaxed?				
Did the presenter answer the audience's questions?				
OVERALL RATING				

Summing Up

Tyrone's Story

Go back to the beginning of this lesson, and reread the story about Tyrone. Then review what you wrote about him, looking at it from his perspective. What did you learn in this lesson that would help him? Imagine that Tyrone has decided to take the position and he has come to you for help in developing his speaking skills. On a separate piece of paper, write a letter to Tyrone in which you give him suggestions for preparing an oral presentation and advice on controlling his nervousness in front of groups.

Be prepared to share your letter with your classmates.

Keeping Track

On a separate piece of paper, answer the following questions. Use what you have learned in this lesson to help you.

1 Name three workplace situations in which you might be required to give an oral presentation.

2 List the six steps involved in planning an oral presentation.

3 How is a presentation that is designed to persuade different from one that is intended to inform?

> *"A man may speak very well in the House of Commons, and fail very completely in the House of Lords. There are two distinct styles requisite...."*
> —Benamin Disraeli, English statesman and novelist

Going Further

- Imagine that, instead of being asked by your supervisor to make an oral presentation to convince your co-workers to follow the safety regulations, you were drafted by your co-workers to present their objections to the safety regulations to a committee of managers. Your job is to convince the management that the three objectionable rules (wearing safety glasses, turning off the power every time a device is touched, and using the new hand tools) are unnecessary and time-consuming, as well as damaging to morale. Be sure to consider the managers' point of view and priorities, and build your argument to show how eliminating the rules would support their goals and the company's bottom line. Outline your presentation, indicating the information you would gather, the arguments you would use, and any visual aids you might require. Be prepared to turn in your outline to your teacher.

■ Think of an important issue affecting American society today, an issue that particularly interests you—for example, gun control, job training, health care, equal pay for women and men, the death penalty, drug control. Then write down three main points that you would like to make regarding this issue in a talk before a large group of people. Decide what images or phrases you would need to use in your talk to get your points across effectively. Use phrases that best express your own feelings. Finally, write a three-minute speech on the issue—or make notes for a speech, if you prefer to speak from notes. Be prepared to present your talk to the class.

Education and Earnings: The Gender Gap		
1992 median earnings of full-time employees aged 25 years and older		
Education Level	**Women**	**Men**
High school diploma	$18,648	$26,766
Associate's degree	24,849	32,349
Bachelor's degree	29,284	40,381
Master's degree	35,018	47,260
—United States Census Bureau		

■ Suppose that Dr. Martin Luther King, Jr., had been invited to address a meeting of southern businessmen who were strongly opposed to ending racial segregation in schools. Assume that he would deliver essentially the same message that he expressed in the "I Have a Dream" speech, promoting equality and brotherhood, but this time he would try to convince the "unbelievers" to join in the struggle. He would need to acknowledge their feelings and present his ideas in terms that focus on the benefits that equality will bring to them.

Rewrite Dr. King's speech as you think he would have adapted it for this very different group of listeners. Be prepared to deliver the speech to your classmates and to turn it in to your teacher.

Writing a Persuasive Memo

A Concept Lesson

Looking Ahead

What This Lesson Is About

In this lesson, you will learn how to write persuasively. Being able to express your views in written form is an important asset in the workplace.

✔ A memo (or memorandum) is a brief written message that is exchanged among personnel within a company or organization. Memos may be informational, but they are often designed to inspire action.

✔ Memos usually follow a standard format, and their tone may differ, depending on whether they are sent from a supervisor to an employee or from an employee to the supervisor.

✔ Understanding how to structure your writing to convince the reader will help you write any workplace document that is intended to present a point of view and to motivate your reader to take action.

On Second Thought, Type It Yourself

Number of U.S. Secretaries (in millions)

1984 '86 '88 '90 '92 '93

Source: Bureau of Labor Statistics

Key Ideas

active voice—a sentence structure that emphasizes the actor ("Tiffany threw the ball.")

passive voice—a sentence structure that emphasizes the object of the action ("The ball was thrown by Tiffany.")

A Great Idea for Mr. Johnson

Krista Chang has landed a job with a heating and cooling business. Her boss, Mr. Johnson, who owns the firm, is out of the office much of the day, installing air conditioners and furnaces with his crews. This is Krista's first job, and the only instructions she has received from Mr. Johnson are to answer the phone and take messages. He returns the customers' calls when he gets back in the afternoon.

After several weeks, Krista realizes that she could make a bigger contribution to the company by using the phone to call local residents to solicit business. If sales and installations increase, Mr. Johnson could hire more workers and make more money, and she herself might be given a more responsible position. She wants to tell Mr. Johnson about her idea, but he always seems busy with something else. She decides to write him a memo, which he can read at his convenience.

Imagine that you are Krista Chang. On a separate piece of paper, write out her idea in two or three sentences, which can be used in a memo to Mr. Johnson. Design the statement to persuade Mr. Johnson to give the idea a try.

Be prepared to share your statement with the class.

Getting Started

The Joy of Memorandums

Written communication takes many forms in the workplace. One of the shortest and most widely used forms is the memorandum. Memos work well when you want to communicate formally with your supervisor and co-workers. Unlike most spoken communication, memos can be copied and filed, which enables you to retain a permanent record of your actions. That's an important point to remember. A well-written, thoughtful memo can work to your advantage when your performance is evaluated; on the other hand, a poorly written memo with grammatical and spelling errors can haunt you for years to come.

In most cases, memos are used for comunication between departments in a company. To communicate with co-workers whom you see every day, you would normally speak rather than write. But sometimes you need to put important or complex messages on paper, even when you are sitting at the desk right next to the person to whom you are writing. Or, if you have trouble scheduling a face-to-face meeting with your supervisor or a co-worker, you might use a memo to transmit important information or ideas.

Written messages are particularly useful for giving instructions, setting deadlines, and issuing reminders. You may want to send out a notice of meetings and follow up with a memo summarizing what happened at the meeting.

A memo can be addressed to one person or a number of people (a committee, for example, or all members of a department). Sometimes people other than the ones to whom you send a memo need to know its contents or need to be informed that you have sent it. Give them copies, but don't list their names among the "addressees" at the top of the memo; instead, put their names at the bottom, following "CC:"—sometimes supervisors want to review all memos written by their staff members; at other times, sending a copy is a courtesy.

Writing a Persuasive Memo

Although memos are usually short (one or two pages), they aren't necessarily easy to write. The technique is somewhat like writing a song or a very short story—you put in only the things that will make your point most effectively.

> *"The ability to express oneself in writing is critical to a world-class education."*
>
> —Richard W. Riley,
> United States Secretary
> of Education

STYLE VERSUS SUBSTANCE

GREAT IDEAS CAN BE WRITTEN ON GARBAGE

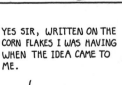

DILBERT reprinted by permission of UFS, Inc.

In general, the writing style of a memo is less formal than that of a letter; sometimes it is even conversational. Use simple, straightforward language, and keep the sentences short. Use the active voice (subject-verb-object, as in "She bought lunch"), rather than the passive voice ("Lunch was bought by her").

The tone of a memo varies, depending on your relationship with the person to whom you are writing. If you are proposing something to your boss, you may choose a somewhat more formal tone than if you are writing to a co-worker. If you are the boss, on the other hand, you can afford to be more directive in giving instructions or assignments than if you are the employee.

Use devices such as "bullets" (large dots) or boldface headings to set off a series of items so that your reader can get the message at a glance. Try to present only one idea per paragraph.

Ten Easy Steps: Here are 10 steps to follow in writing a persuasive memo. You may notice that the steps are similar to those you used in Lesson 10 to create a persuasive oral presentation. As you consider each step, examine the sample memo on page 81 and answer the associated question. Write your answers to these questions on a separate sheet of paper.

1 Decide what you wish to accomplish. What is the thesis, claim, or point of view that you want to state? Write two or three sentences that clearly make your point. Everything else in your memo will develop from or support this point.

In the sample memo on page 81, what is the point that Jane Lane wants to make?

2 Before composing your memo, consider your readers. What do they already know about the topic of your memo? What else do they need to know in order to be persuaded? If they are likely to resist your ideas, try to anticipate and respond to their objections, and point out the benefits that your proposal can bring.

What evidence is there that Jane Lane anticipated objections by her reader? What benefits does she point out?

3 Plan your approach. Will your memo need to sound friendly, stern, or both? What is your relationship to the reader—are you writing to your supervisor, your employees, or your co-worker?

How would you characterize Jane Lane's approach? What words or sentences lead you to say so?

4 Gather all the information you will need in order to say what you want to say in the way you want to say it.

What factual points does Jane Lane include in her memo?

Heading

Addressee, Title
Writer's name, phone
Date
Subject of memo

Body of memo

Main point

Rationale for change

Request

Benefits

Conclusion (call to action)

Others who receive copies of the memo

City General Hospital

MEMORANDUM

TO: Alex Smith, Food Service Director
FROM: Jane Lane, Human Resources (X343)
DATE: October 2, 1996
SUBJ: Cafeteria Menu

Alex, I know that you put a great dealof time and thought into planning the cafeteria menus, and we would all be lost without this service. A number of employees have come to me recently, however, with some suggestions and asked me to pass them on to you.

You may not be aware of two recent changes in our work force:

- We now have employees from many different cultures and nationalities whose food tastes differ from the standard American fair. Some are vegetarians; others do not eat pork.

- The new employee fitness program has made us more concious of cholesterol, fat, and sugar in our diets. Those who are in the Weight Watchers class are expecially concerned about calories.

We hope that you will consider some or all of the following changes in the cafeteria menu:

- More steamed vegetables; more chicken, less pork and beef
- Whole grain instead of white bread
- A wider varity of salads—perhaps a salad bar where employees can choose the ingredients themselves
- Low-fat or diet salad dressings; low-fat oil for cooking

These changes are apprpriate to our mission as "The Hospital of Health." And I'm sure that increase use of the cafeteria will more than make up for any additional costs that may be involved.

Please me with your reactions to these suggestions. Perhaps we could conduct a quick survey of all employees to get a more complete sense of their preferences. I'd be glad to work with you on that, if you wish.

CC: Juan Espinosa, Director, Human Resources
       Akiko Yamaha, Staff Council

5 Conclude your memo with a request or suggestion for follow-up or action.

What does Jane Lane suggest as the next step?

6 If you are sending copies of the memo to other people, list them at the end of the memo after "CC:" ("CC" originally meant "carbon copy"; today photocopies are much more common, but the "CC" is still used.)

Who will receive copies of Jane Lane's memo? Why do you think she is sending copies to them?

7 Write a first draft. Use no unnecessary words.

8 Test and revise. Have someone you trust read and criticize your first draft. Reread it yourself, then write a second draft and make whatever changes are necessary.

9 Double-check your facts, and proofread your second draft for grammar, punctuation, and spelling.

What grammar or spelling errors can you find in Jane Lane's memo?

10 Make a final draft, and distribute your memo.

Be prepared to discuss these 10 steps and your answers to the questions about Jane Lane's memo with the class.

> *"If writing must be a precise form of communication, it should be treated like a precision instrument. It should be sharpened and it should not be used carelessly."*
>
> —Theodore M. Bernstein, American journalist and wordsmith

Trying It Out

A Parking Problem

Jane Lane wrote a pretty good memo—even though she did make some typographical and spelling errors. But Ed Rable, who is a section head in the shipping department of a company, really needs help. First of all, he's fighting mad about the building committee's decision to close down the employee parking lot. He also really doesn't know how to write a convincing memo of protest. He realizes that, in its present state, his memo won't get much attention, so he has come to you for advice. You agree to revise it for him.

Here is Ed's first draft of his memo:

MEMORANDUM

TO: Building Committee

FROM: Ed Rable

DATE: [Use today's date]

SUBJ: Parking Changes

Closing Parking Lot A of our plant is the most ludicrous idea I have heard of in the 21 years I have worked for Consolidated Widgets. I can't believe our executive committee would buy such a pig in the poke idea as closing the lot to put in a flower garden. This is just as bad as when we changed from gasoline to battery powered forklifts in the warehouse, which our employees always forget to charge the batteries and so the forklifts run out of power just when you have a rush order to get out the door. I trust you will reconsider the flower garden which would be a great inconvenience to the many employees who have to get to work here on time or else be docked their pay.

The current Lot A is right next to the shipping dock and as such is convenient for most employees who work on the west side of the plant. Moving the lot to Spencer Street would force employees to walk three blocks to the plant when right now they can step out of their cars and be inside in a minute or two. Given the rotten winters we have in this neck of the woods, it is a bad deal to have to go so far to get a parking space, of which we never have enough to go around as it is.

We need parking spaces not decoration here, even though some nice grass and plants would spruce up the factory.

> ### How Much Would You Pay for a Parking Space?
>
> The costs of creating one parking space range from $2,000 to $5,000 for a surface lot, and as high as $10,000 to $12,000 in a two- or three-story structure....Costs vary widely by location, but can be calculated from the local cost for an acre of land: A parking space takes up 340 square feet for both the space and the aisle. There are about 128 spaces per acre.
>
> —Adapted from "Turning Asphalt into Biomass," *IBF News* (1993)

Taking advantage of what you have learned in this lesson, rewrite Ed's memo. Use Jane Lane's memo (without the typographical and spelling errors) as a model for your work. Remember that Ed's memo is going from an employee to a management committee, and he doesn't want to offend the bosses—but he also doesn't want them to close that parking lot.

When you have completed your re-draft, exchange your work with a classmate, and use a copy of the **Persuasive Writing Checklist** to give each other feedback. What's good? What's not so good? What changes should be made?

Then revise your memo, incorporating the suggestions that you think will improve it.

Keep a copy of your memo in your portfolio.

Persuasive Writing Checklist

Element	Yes	No	Suggestions
Is the purpose clear?			
Is the main point clearly expressed?			
Is sufficient evidence presented?			
Is the argument convincing and logical?			
Is the writing style appropriate?			
Is the language simple and written in the active voice?			
Is it correct in spelling and grammar?			
Is there a call for action?			
Does the memo follow the standard format?			
Are graphic devices (bullets, boldface) used to highlight the main points?			
If you received this memo, would you be convinced to follow the recommendations?			
OVERALL RATING			

Summing Up

Giving Feedback to Ed

You know that Ed wants to get the memo off to the building committee next week, and you're afraid he may be upset by all your changes. You'd like to discuss them with him in person, but there's no time because you're leaving after work for a week's vacation.

■ Draft a memo to Ed explaining what you changed and why. Knowing that he may be sensitive about what you have done, be sure to work in one or two compliments about his original memo, if you can. Exchange this memo with a different classmate, and repeat the feedback process, using another copy of the **Persuasive Writing Checklist.**

Revise your memo on the basis of the feedback.

> *"Planning to write is not writing. Outlining...researching...talking to people about what you're doing, none of that is writing. Writing is writing."*
>
> —E. L. Doctorow, American novelist

Keeping Track

On a separate sheet of paper, answer the following questions. Use what you have learned in this lesson to help you.

1 Why are some memos classified as a type of persuasive writing?

2 How does the writing style and tone of a memo differ from that of a letter? What is the usual audience for a memo? For a letter?

3 List at least three rules for writing effective persuasive memos.

Going Further

■ Try writing your own memorandum. Suppose that, as a student, you think some aspects of your school's policies are unfair and are damaging student morale. Write a memo to your principal outlining your objections and suggesting ways to improve the atmosphere for learning. Suggest one of the following changes in school policy, or think of your own example:

- Require teachers to make flexible homework assignments, with students doing only as many problems as necessary to show that they know how to do them instead of repeating the same kind of exercise over and over.

- Allow students to make up all missed or late assignments without penalty.

- Have students fill out written evaluations of teachers for use in determining salaries and promotions.

Remember that you are addressing an adult who is also the top authority figure in your school. Build your argument carefully, and remember to point out the advantages for the school, the principal, and the teachers, as well as for the students. Follow the format of Jane Lane's memo on page 81. Be prepared to share your memo with the class and to turn it in to your teacher.

■ Several software programs to help you construct business letters and memos are available. If you have access to one, try using it to complete one or more of the assignments in this lesson. Then write a one-page review of the program, pointing out the ways in which it helped or failed to help you complete your task. Be prepared to turn in your review to your teacher.

■ Think of someone whom you would like to persuade to do something—for example, a member of Congress to vote for a piece of legislation, or your favorite rap star to do a concert in your city. Write this person a letter expressing your beliefs and feelings on the matter and urging him or her to do as you request. Make it as persuasive as you can. Be prepared to share your letter with the class and with your teacher.

Do Your Own Thing

"That was an awesome catch," the football announcer yelled into the microphone. "Brown is having a huge game tonight...."

If you're a sports fan, you've heard sportscasters use the words "awesome" and "huge" game after game, week after week. They have turned these words into cliches.

A cliche is an expression that is overused to the point that it becomes stale and loses its force. The first announcer who described some athlete's performance as "awesome" was actually using that word in a clever, new way. He was adding an adjective to the vocabulary of sports. Unfortunately, the word caught on with so many other sportscasters that it soon sounded worn out and trite instead of clever and fresh.

Cliches are like fads. They come and go, just like the latest crazes in food and clothing. Do you like to "do your own thing"? Are you trying to maintain a "high profile" at school? Do you know anyone who still says "That's not my bag"? All these cliches used to be very popular. But they are fading away, and guess what—nobody seems to mind. That's because after a while cliches get boring. People get tired of them.

So here's the deal. Don't just go with the flow and repeat the same tired cliches all the time. Build up your vocabulary. The English language is full of good words that can express your meaning clearly and creatively. Don't get uptight over this. Go for it.

Negotiating with Supervisors

A Concept Lesson

Looking Ahead

What This Lesson Is About

In this lesson, you will learn how to deal with feedback that you receive in the workplace about your performance, behavior, and attitude. You will also learn how to negotiate with supervisors about issues of pay, benefits, and work load.

✔ No one enjoys being criticized, but knowing how to respond positively to criticism can make the difference between being promoted and being fired.

✔ At other times, you may need to meet with your supervisor to discuss a raise in pay or a promotion—or your supervisor may ask you to take on more work during a busy period or when downsizing reduces the work force.

✔ Seven basic negotiating techniques can help you resolve differences with supervisors in a positive way, which can benefit both you and your employer.

How you respond to criticism will affect both your relationship with your supervisor and your performance on the job.

87

Key Ideas

downsizing—reduction in size of the work force, usually because of the loss of business income or a general downturn in the economy

job description—a statement of duties and desired performance levels for a specified position in the workplace

negotiation—a process for resolving differences and reaching agreement through discussion and bargaining

performance review or job evaluation—a formal process for determining an employee's progress

Handling Criticism

"Bryan, your room is a pig sty. Only you would store half-eaten peanut butter sandwiches under the bed!"

"Hey, Renée, are you going to make some more of those 'jawbreaker' cookies for the party tonight?"

"Milton, this paper doesn't even deserve the 'C' I gave it. You missed the point entirely, and you misspelled more words than you spelled correctly."

Do any of these remarks sound familiar? The world can be cruel when we don't measure up to its standards—and that's true in the workplace too. How painful the criticism is depends on who gives it and whether it appears to be valid.

> *"Criticism, as it was first instituted by [the Greek philosopher] Aristotle, was meant as a standard of judging well."*
>
> —Samuel Johnson, English lexicographer, essayist, and poet

- Bryan is probably tired of hearing complaints from his mother about his room, but he knows he's a slob, and keeping his room clean isn't a high priority with him.

- Renée may feel the sting more deeply. She was proud of those cookies. They were a little hard, but that was the recipe's fault.

- Milton is crushed—and angry! He worked hard on the paper, and he thought he had done a great job. He tosses his paper in the waste can and convinces himself that the teacher hates him.

These are not model reactions to criticism, but they are common ones. They are also responses that don't go over well in the workplace.

■ Think of a time when you were criticized—by a parent, a teacher, a supervisor, or one of your friends. What was **your** response? Did you do anything to improve the situation? Did you learn anything from the criticism? In your journal, describe the incident and answer the preceding questions.

88

Getting Started

Talking with a Supervisor

Just as teachers grade your work to let you know how you're doing, employers evaluate your performance on the job. Sometimes this takes place through regular performance reviews or job evaluations. Not all employers make these formal assessments, but there is always feedback of some kind, even if it's just a pat on the back and a "Good job!"—or a warning such as "You'd better shape up, or you'll be shipping out." Between the two extremes is the employer who sits down from time to time with each employee, discusses his or her performance, and offers suggestions for improvement.

Other times when you may have differences with your supervisor occur when you ask for a raise, a promotion, extra days off, or a transfer to another department—or when the employer asks you to take on additional work, to speed up your productivity, or to accept a demotion because the company is downsizing.

In all of these situations, good communication skills are essential, and knowing how to negotiate positively is a definite "plus."

How to Negotiate

Negotiation is a process by which people use communication to resolve differences and reach agreement. The best resolutions are "win-win" situations, in which both sides gain something.

Even if your supervisor is not a skilled negotiator, your use of a few simple strategies can move the meeting out of an uncomfortable standoff into a discussion that can result in benefits to both of you. These strategies are:

1. **Listen actively.** Force yourself to get beyond your feeling of anger or hurt when you are being criticized—or the resentment you feel for not being paid enough or for being asked to do more work. Such emotions will keep you from hearing what your supervisor is saying, both in words and in body language. Listen for clues that will tell you what is important to the supervisor and the company, what is expected of you, and in what ways you have failed to meet expectations.

2. **Try to understand the supervisor's point of view.** Is there pressure to increase productivity or profit? Is the criticism a way of helping you improve your skills? Are you seen as part of the problem—or part of the solution? Present your suggestions in terms of the employer's needs, not your own. (For example, if you are asking for a "flex-time" schedule, which allows employees to set their own work hours as long as they put in the required time, say: "This will allow the phones to remain open for two more hours every day, and flexible hours will reduce stress and make workers more

89

productive." Do **not** say, "Some of us hate to get up early in the morning. With flex time, we can sleep in and not be late for work so often.")

3 **Show concern for the supervisor's point of view.** Let the supervisor know you understand that he or she is responsible for managing the budget and for seeing that everybody does a good job. Make it clear that you are not thinking only of yourself.

4 **Focus on common interests.** Point out that, just as the company wants and needs good employees, you want to be a good worker, you want to contribute to the company's success, and you are willing to make an extra effort to improve your skills or your work habits.

5 **Invent new options.** If the issue is your evaluation, ask for help in identifying resources to help you improve in your areas of weakness. If you are willing to take an evening course, for example, would the company be willing to pay the fees? If the issue is a raise, perhaps you can suggest a small increase now and a second one in six months—or in exchange for the raise, perhaps you could take on additional duties.

6 **Agree on what is fair to both sides.** If you are being asked to do more work without additional pay, it might be fair to ask for extra vacation time or increased benefits. If you agree to carry an additional load during a financial crisis, it might be fair to ask to participate in the profit-sharing plan when the crisis is over.

7 **Know your walk-away options.** If all else fails, you can always leave the job. But before you do that—or even suggest it as a possibility—be sure that you know what options you have. Are there other jobs open in your area? Is the pay comparable to what you are making? Can you afford to be without a job for weeks or even months?

Have a Problem? Make a Suggestion

If your supervisor seems irritated when you mention a problem at work, you may believe that she doesn't want to be bothered. In fact, the opposite is probably true. Your supervisor probably **does** want to know about problems in your work environment. What she is likely to find irritating, however, are employees who appear to rely on her to resolve their problems, without offering any possible solutions on their own. To avoid giving your supervisor this impression, be prepared to offer a solution if you run into a problem at work. You can turn a problem into an opportunity to show your problem-solving skills.

In the next section, you will try out these strategies by playing roles in several scenarios that involve an employee and a supervisor. First, though, review the steps to be sure you understand them. Then analyze the following five quotations, which are from employees who are meeting with their supervisors.

Write the numbers 1 through 5 on a separate sheet of paper; beside each of these quotation numbers, write the numbers of any of the seven negotiation steps to which each quotation relates; also state whether the speaker is using or ignoring the negotiation steps.

1 "I need a raise because we're expecting a baby, the rent is going up, and we can barely get by on what I'm making now."

2 "I understand, with the cutback in funding, why you are asking me to take on 10 more clients every week, but I'm already feeling overloaded. I'm afraid that the quality of our service will drop if we try to do too much. Couldn't we look into getting some student interns from the college? They could handle a lot of the paperwork, and then we would have time to serve more clients."

3 "If you're not satisfied with the way I'm doing my job, I'll just have to quit. I'm doing the best I can."

4 "I really don't think it's fair to keep me at my starting salary for two years. If you think a 10 percent raise is too high, would you consider five percent now and, perhaps, an additional three percent in June, when we have our annual reviews?"

> *"To avoid criticism, do nothing, say nothing, be nothing."*
> —Elbert Hubbard, American businessman, writer, and printer

5 (In tears) "I just feel terrible that you don't like my work. I've always been an 'A' student, and I think the report I did was fine. You don't care, do you? You just want to get rid of me."

Be prepared to discuss your answers with your classmates.

Trying It Out

How Would You Handle These Situations?

You are about to read three brief scenarios of meetings between a supervisor and an employee. Pair up with a classmate; choose one of the scenarios; and plan the dialogue that takes place between the two people.

Use what you have learned about negotiating in this lesson to turn the problem into a "win-win" situation. Be prepared to perform your scenario for the class. You may change the gender and name of either character to reflect the gender of the "actors."

91

No Monkey Business Here

Portia has worked for two months, helping to feed and care for the animals at a small zoo. She likes the job because she has always loved animals, but she hates to clean the cages and sometimes forgets to do so. She also gets very nervous when visitors ask her questions about the animals because she's had no veterinary training. She's more at home talking to the animals than to people anyway.

When the zookeeper, Mr. Santora, discovers that the monkey cage once again has not been cleaned—this marks the third time in three weeks—he calls Portia into his office.

■ Act out the conversation that takes place between Portia and Mr. Santora.

No Place Like Home

Eduardo is a designer for a small but rapidly growing software company. He does much of his work alone. Other workers then test the programs and give them back to Eduardo for revisions. He's good at what he does, and he spends a lot of time working at home on his own computer system, experimenting with his latest ideas.

Getting to work on time, however, is a big problem. He lives 20 miles away from the office; he doesn't have a car; and the buses run very irregularly. He has been reprimanded several times for being late, with the threat that if it continues, his pay will be docked for the hours he misses.

Eduardo has an idea for solving the problem. He makes an appointment with his boss, Miss Shen, to present his proposal.

■ Assume the roles of Eduardo and Miss Shen, and play out their conversation.

Pitching In

Times are tough for Southside Community Services, Inc. The social service agency provides day care for children and senior adults, operates a food bank, and offers job and education counseling to low-income families in an economically depressed neighborhood. Two major funding sources have cut back their support, and the executive director, Mrs. Washington, was forced to lay off three employees. She kept Luisa, the job counselor, because she had the highest placement rate of anyone on staff. Now, however, she has to give her the bad news: She will have to take a 10 percent pay cut and increase her caseload.

Luisa likes her job—and needs it. She's a single mother with a two-year-old child in day care, and she's responsible for her elderly grandmother, who will soon need to be in a day program for seniors. That will be an additional expense. She can't afford a pay cut, but she can't afford to lose her job either.

■ Role-play the conversation between Luisa and the executive director, Mrs. Washington.

As you watch your classmates perform their scenarios, rate their negotiating skills by completing a copy of the **Negotiation Feedback** form. Your classmates will rate you in the same manner when you perform.

After each pair has reviewed the feedback forms, take a few minutes to discuss the performances. Did the various players use negotiating strategies? Was the outcome a "win-win" situation? How could the interactions have been improved?

Caring for Elderly Relatives

By the year 2050, the number of Americans caring for frail relatives could double or triple the number providing such care in 1990. The 1990 Census revealed that for white, non-Hispanic Americans, there were 23 persons 80 years old or older for every 100 persons who were 50 to 64 years old. By the year 2050, that population group may have as many as 58 persons 80 years old or older for every 100 persons who are 50 to 64 years old. The table below shows how this ratio could change for other population groups.

Persons 80 or older per 100 Persons 50–64

Population Group	1990	2050
White, non-Hispanic	23	58
Black	16	27
American Indian, Eskimo, and Aleut	11	38
Asian and Pacific Islander	9	34
Hispanic	11	36

Note: Persons of Hispanic origin may be of any race.

—United States Census Bureau

Negotiation Feedback

Role Players: _____

Your Name: _____

Strategy	Yes	No	Suggested Improvements
LISTENING:			
Did the employee listen actively?			
Did the employer listen actively?			
UNDERSTANDING:			
Did the employee try to understand the other side?			
Did the employer try to understand the other side?			
CONCERN:			
Did the employee show concern?			
Did the employer show concern?			
FOCUS ON INTERESTS:			
Did the employee focus on common interests?			
Did the employer focus on common interests?			
NEW OPTIONS:			
Did they explore new options?			
FAIRNESS:			
Was the outcome fair to both sides?			
WALK-AWAY OPTIONS:			
Did the employee consider his/her walk-away options?			
Was the resolution a "win-win" situation?			
SUMMARY: How would you have handled the discussion differently?			

Summing Up

An Uneven Playing Field

When you have differences with a brother, a sister, a friend, or a co-worker, you're on pretty even ground. It's usually easier to negotiate when neither party has any real authority or power over the other one.

But when you differ with a parent or a boss, it's a whole different story. As much as you may resent it, your parents do have some control over what you do and where you go. They can punish you—or simply say no. Supervisors have even more authority within the workplace. They can require you to do certain things, and they can recommend—or advise against—a raise or promotion. They can even fire you.

So what's the point of trying to negotiate with authority figures? Simple. They happen to be human beings too—and most of them respond to positive, helpful attitudes and indications that you understand the whole picture, not just your own wants and needs. Most supervisors want you to succeed, and most are more than willing to help.

She's sure she told you to update the program notes. You remember no such discussion. Your best strategy is to avoid arguing over who *should* have done it and to focus on negotiating a way to do it.

Using the skills you learned in this lesson will help you to demonstrate a positive attitude and a willingness to work harder to overcome your inexperience or your areas of weakness. That can make a big difference with most supervisors. And if you have a boss who doesn't respond to your positive attitude, you have nothing to lose by trying it. Even if you find that you have to use your walk-away option and leave, you will be leaving on friendly terms, with a better chance of getting a good recommendation for future jobs.

Keeping Track

On a separate piece of paper, answer the following questions. Use what you have learned in this lesson to help you.

1 What are three situations in which negotiation skills can help an employee communicate effectively with a supervisor?

2 Why is it important to listen actively and to try to understand the supervisor's point of view?

3 What are two questions that you need to consider before you exercise your "walk-away" option and leave a job?

Going Further

■ Interview an employed parent, relative, or friend who reports to a supervisor on the job. Also interview another person whose job involves supervising other workers. Ask each of them how performance is reviewed and evaluated and how they, as individuals, respond to criticism or suggestions that their work needs improvement. (Remember that most supervisors also have superiors who evaluate them!) Ask the person in a nonsupervisory position how he or she would ask for a raise or a promotion; then ask how he or she would deal with a demotion or pay cut. Ask the supervisor what response he or she hopes to see in an employee who is given constructive criticism; also ask what he or she considers an appropriate way for an employee to ask for a raise or additional benefits. Compare the response you receive with what you have learned in this lesson. Point out any negotiating strategies that your interviewees mentioned. (Perhaps your contact won't use the term "negotiation," but you will be able to recognize the strategy from what you have learned.) Summarize your comparison in a one- or two-page paper, and turn it in to your teacher.

■ Assume that you have been asked to contribute a chapter to an employee manual on "How to Talk to Your Supervisor." Review what you have learned in this lesson, and, using the research and organizing skills you developed in Lessons 10 and 11, outline the chapter. Share your outline with several classmates for feedback. Then fill in the outline by writing the chapter. Be prepared to share your finished work with the class and your teacher.

■ Even young children can benefit from learning the principles of negotiation. Think about the seven strategies for resolving differences, and translate them into terms that an elementary school child could understand. Be sure to use words and examples that children can understand and relate to. Then develop a children's book based on the strategies. You may make it a simple guide or turn it into a story, with some characters using the appropriate strategies and others getting into trouble because they do not use them. Illustrate your book with drawings or computer clip-art (illustrations available in a computer program). Recruit several children in your family or neighborhood to critique your book, and revise it to incorporate the suggestions that you think are good. Be prepared to share your completed book with the class and your teacher. Keep it in your portfolio.

Just Like Family?

In my work, I see many people who are under a great deal of stress due to a strained relationship with their boss. In terms of how it affects them, most people's relationship with their boss is second only to their relationship with their immediate family.

—Boyd Sturdevant, owner and director of Employee Counseling of Indiana

Electronic Communication

A Concept Lesson

Looking Ahead

What This Lesson Is About

In this lesson, you will learn about writing electronic mail, or e-mail, in the workplace. As an employee, you will be responsible for using your company's e-mail system in a professional manner.

☑ Effective e-mail messages are well-written, brief, and courteous.

☑ To use e-mail effectively in the workplace, follow the rules of e-mail etiquette.

☑ Avoid "flaming" or confrontational messages that might hurt or anger other persons or might have serious consequences for you and your employer.

GARY "THE GROUCH" GILLMAN HAD A CUSTOMIZED INTERNET KEYBOARD...

FLAME

COVERLY

Key Ideas

electronic mail or e-mail—a written message transmitted by computer on an electronic network

etiquette—procedures prescribed to achieve smooth social relations

flame—to make inflammatory or hurtful statements in an e-mail message; a confrontational e-mail message

Parking Privileges

Imagine that you are a new employee working in an office building that has a big parking lot. You're running late one cold and rainy Monday morning, and as you pull into the lot you see an open space near the entrance. As you head toward it, a co-worker in a fancy sports car beats you to the spot. You were right in front of him—he must have seen you—but he hops out of his car and scurries into the building without casting a glance in your direction. You eventually find a spot at the rear of the lot and walk through the rain to the entrance. You're not only cold and wet, you're also angry.

Your new employer has an electronic mail system, which means you can instantly give your co-worker a piece of your mind, without having to say it to his face. You compose a blistering complaint and, with great satisfaction, send it to your fellow worker's e-mail address.

■ On a separate piece of paper, answer the following question:

- What would you write in your e-mail message to the co-worker who beat you to the parking space and then snubbed you? Make a list of the things you might say.

■ Now consider the following questions:

- What if, after sending the e-mail, you learn that the person you thought was a space grabber had just been named the company's "Employee of the Month" and that the space has been reserved for him as a reward? What would your co-worker think about you and your e-mail message? How would you feel?

Be prepared to share your responses with the class.

> *"One man was so mad at me that he ended his letter: 'Beware. You will never get out of this world alive.'"*
>
> —John Steinbeck, American author

Getting Started

E-Mail in the Workplace

Electronic mail is a cross between a letter and a phone call. It is a written document, but it is transmitted electronically. Instead of sending a handwritten or typed piece of paper through regular mail or by fax machine, you type your message on a computer and transmit it on an electronic network. In a split second your message goes to one person or to as many people as you choose. The network may serve only your workplace, or it may reach to the other side of the world.

Effective e-mail messages are well-written, brief, and courteous. They follow the same general rules used in all good writing. But e-mail users often write hastily, and their messages may take on a conversational tone. They may use words that have more than one meaning and can be misinterpreted.

Because you can't see or hear the person who receives your e-mail message, it's also easy to "shoot from the hip" and write things that you wouldn't say in person. Such hurtful and angry messages are described as "flaming." It is best to avoid writing flaming messages that could have serious consequences for the sender and the receiver, as well as the company or companies that employ them. Flaming messages may result not only in embarrassment and hurt feelings but also in reprimands or firings. They might even foul up your company's relations with another company.

To help ensure that your e-mail messages are written and understood correctly, you can follow three simple rules for responsible e-mail behavior. Think of them as the rules of "E-mail Etiquette."

- ■ **Discuss one topic.** E-mail is best used for quick and urgent communication on a specific topic. Be sure your message covers only that topic. If you have several subjects to discuss, present each one in a separate message.

- ■ **Be brief.** It is best to use short words, sentences, and paragraphs. Keep your overall message brief too. If it takes more than 20 or 30 lines on your computer screen, send a memo instead.

- ■ **Be courteous.** Above all, don't flame. Flaming is the most common e-mail blunder. Before you send a flame, stop and ask yourself, "Would I say this to someone face-to-face?" If not, revise your message.

These rules are adapted from J. Goode and M. Johnson's article "Putting Out the Flames: The Etiquette and Law of E-Mail," *Online* (November 1991). Reprinted by permission of Online, Inc.

E-mail Etiquette

Along with the rules of etiquette described in **Getting Started**, courteous and responsible e-mail users also follow these rules of behavior:

- Don't "flame!" A flame is a nasty or obnoxious e-mail message. This is the most common e-mail blunder. Before you send an angry message, stop and think. Ask yourself, "Would I say this to someone face-to-face?" If not, revise your message.

- Don't forward a personal message without permission. Forwarding means passing on a message from one person to readers who were not intended to receive it. Don't forward e-mail unless you ask the sender first.

- Most people receive lots of e-mail. Don't clog up their accounts with unnecessary messages. These often go unread!

- Don't abuse a company system with personal messages or advertisements.

— Adapted from J. Goode and M. Johnson, "Putting Out the Flames: The Etiquette and Law of E-mail," *Online* (November 1991). Reprinted with permission of Online, Inc.

Now take a few minutes to answer the following questions. Be prepared to share your answers with the class.

1 How is e-mail like a letter? How is it like a phone call?

2 Have you ever used e-mail? If so, with whom have you communicated, and what subjects have you discussed?

3 What are the characteristics of effective e-mail messages?

4 Why would employees be tempted to send hurtful or angry messages by e-mail when they would never say the same things face-to-face?

"GOOD LORD, CONROY...IT'S A MESSAGE FROM UNCLE SAM!"

Trying It Out

Flares and Flames

Sometimes, if you're very upset or angry, you may be tempted to write a flaming e-mail message just to get it off your chest—and then trash it in the computer's garbage can. No harm done, right? As a matter of fact, this is a very dangerous thing to do, because the message could still get away from you. Many systems store trashed messages for at least a day; therefore, it would be easy for someone else on the network to read your message and perhaps send it on deliberately or tell the other person about it. You could even accidentally send it yourself—and once you've given the command, it's gone!

There are better and safer ways to vent your anger: Take a walk; work out in the exercise room; or treat yourself to a soft drink or a candy bar. If you **must** write down your thoughts to let off steam, do it on paper and then tear it up.

On the other hand, there's nothing wrong with using e-mail to relay complaints or to call attention to a problem. Just be cool when you do it, even if this means waiting a day until the "flame" is down to a flicker. The following paragraphs contain an example of an e-mail message that should not be sent. Tony is furious—and he has a right to be—but is there a better way for him to deal with the problem?

Tony Is Ticked

Tony Santiago works for a company that manufactures electronic equipment. It's a highly competitive market, and to maintain a reasonable profit margin, the company has been forced to come up with a way to produce more goods in less time without reducing the quality. Tony and several other employees recently attended a workshop in Total Quality Management, and they are looking for ways to use the TQM approach. There's no time during the workday when they can meet, so they've agreed to come in an hour early every Tuesday morning to do their brainstorming.

The problem is that the company-sponsored aerobics class meets Monday evenings in the same conference room that Tony's group uses. The instructor, Hank "Macho-Man" Bergermeister, shoves all the furniture to one side and frequently forgets to put it back. Tony, who isn't getting paid for the extra hour he's spending with his work group, is offended that **he** has to move the furniture back and clean up after Macho-Man at 7 o'clock in the morning. The third time it happens he blows up. As soon as his meeting is over, he goes straight to his computer and types this e-mail message to his supervisor:

DATE: 10/24/96   livingston@linknet.com

TO: J. Livingston

FROM: T. Santiago

SUBJ: Bergermeister's Mess

I'm sick of coming in at 7 a.m. on Tuesdays to rearrange the conference room. For the third straight week, Macho-Man (who, of course, can do no wrong) high-tailed it out of here after his aerobics group, leaving the furniture piled in the corner and mats on the floor. I'm in here, on my own time, setting up the TQM meeting, but first I have to move furniture. Who does Bergermeister think he is, anyway?

It's time this company decided where its priorities are. Do you want to get a TQM program up and running—or is employee bodybuilding your goal? If I have to clean up his mess one more time, you can forget your TQM.

Okay, Tony. We know how you feel. But are you sure you want to send this message?

Discuss Tony's problem and what he should do about it. Some of the questions you may want to consider are:

- How will the supervisor react to the e-mail message?

- How will he feel about Tony—and about Hank—after he reads it?

- Will this get the problem solved?

- Should Tony be complaining to the supervisor—or to Hank directly?

- Total Quality Management stresses teamwork and cooperation. What will this memo say about Tony's understanding of TQM?

- If the supervisor speaks to Hank about the problem, what effect will that have on Tony and Hank's relationship on the job?

- What is the problem? What is a possible solution?

When you have finished your discussion, work together to write a better e-mail message for Tony to send. Decide who should receive it, what its tone should be, and what solution (if any) should be proposed. Compose the message that you would send if you were Tony.

Be prepared to share your answers and your e-mail message with the class.

Summing Up

Thinking about the Consequences

People who send flaming e-mail messages don't usually think about the consequences of what they are doing. Often they don't even learn about the consequences—the recipient of a flaming message might simply ignore it or feel hurt but say nothing about it.

At other times the message brings an even angrier response. And sometimes the sender's supervisor gets involved. The consequences can embarrass and even cause permanent damage to the sender.

Keep in mind the possible consequences of "blowing off steam," whether it is by e-mail, face-to-face, or over the telephone. Popping off usually just makes things worse. It's like throwing gasoline on a fire.

- Using what you have learned in this lesson, write a brief and persuasive e-mail message that a supervisor might send to employees, outlining the rules of etiquette they should follow when they use e-mail.

Be prepared to share your messages with the class.

Keeping Track

On a separate piece of paper, answer the following questions. Use what you have learned in this lesson to help you.

1 What are three characteristics of effective e-mail messages?

2 Why is it important to follow e-mail etiquette in the workplace?

3 Why is the e-mail etiquette rule against sending flaming messages important?

One Final Word of Caution

Whether you are writing a memo, answering a customer's phone call, or sending a message to a co-worker by e-mail, never forget that the person receiving your message is a human being. Especially if your message is something the other person doesn't want to hear, you should be careful to use words that invite discussion, not anger. A few words sent in anger may make you satisfied for a moment, but they could come back to haunt you for a long time.

Going Further

- Practice your e-mail writing skills. Read the following scenarios, then create a well-written, brief, and courteous e-mail message responding to one of them. Be prepared to share your message with the class and your teacher.

    You are Victor Freed, manager of a photo lab at a big-city newspaper. Your staff processes film and prints photos for publication. A busy freelance photographer, Martin Russell, sends in a roll of film containing pictures for a major feature story, but the film comes up blank in the developing process. You need to inform

103

Russell as quickly as possible and find out whether he has other photos that the newspaper can use. You know you can reach him at russell@linknet.com (his e-mail address).

Emily Chang is a data entry clerk for an insurance company. Her computer room is used around the clock by three shifts of keypunch operators. No food or drink is allowed in the room, but somebody at her workstation has been ignoring the rules. For the past few days, she has arrived at work to find the keyboard surrounded by bits of greasy potato chips. She figures they must have been dropped by the operator on the shift just before hers. She sends an e-mail message to her department head, Lawanda Wilcox, at wilcox@linknet.com (her e-mail address).

■ Individually or in groups, visit an office in your school or at a local business that has a computer link used for sending e-mail messages. Have the computer operator show you how the system operates and how actual e-mail messages look. Find out whether the e-mail writers observe the rules of etiquette that you learned in this lesson. Be prepared to share your information with the class and your teacher.

An Electronics Career

"Electronics is the nation's largest manufacturing sector, with approximately 2.3 million American workers employed directly in the industry. Worldwide sales of electronics firms now total over $400 billion per year. Moreover, as the tool builder for the rest of the economy, the U.S. electronics industry certainly would rank very high, if not number one in strategic importance for the economic well-being of the U.S."

—Robert J. Saldich, chairman of the board of the American Electronics Association, during a 1993 Senate hearing on U.S.-Japan trade negotiations

Keeping the Line Running

A Literature Lesson

Looking Ahead

What This Lesson Is About

In this lesson, you will read an article based on an interview with a spot-welder who works at a Chicago automobile assembly plant. His job is primarily to do his part to keep the assembly line running, a task that he finds stressful and dehumanizing.

✔ The environment in an industrial workplace can be stressful for workers, who may be torn between their feelings as human beings and the robotlike behavior required of them.

✔ In such an environment, relations between supervisors and workers are often strained.

✔ Even in this dehumanizing environment, a worker can find ways to survive.

The steady, unrelenting pace of an assembly line can make you feel more like a robot than a person.

Over and Over Again

Have you ever performed a task that was extremely repetitive, such as shucking corn by hand all day or adding columns of numbers or stuffing goods into bags or hammering nails or shifting piles of paper? How did this monotonous activity make you feel? What did you think about as you did it? Were other persons doing the same task? What were their reactions?

In your journal, describe this activity and how you and other persons reacted to it.

Be prepared to share your writing with the class and to compare descriptions. Do other students' descriptions have any similarities to yours? Make a list of words or phrases that two or more students used to describe their experiences. Save the list for use later in this lesson.

Getting Started

"Phil Stallings" by Studs Terkel

The following selection, though written from the first-person or "I" point of view, is based on an interview conducted more than two decades ago by Studs Terkel, a Chicago writer. Terkel interviewed Phil Stallings, a spot-welder at a Ford automobile assembly plant.

The article, published in Terkel's 1972 book *Working*, gives a sense of what it is like to be employed in the old-style, mass-production workplace. Ford Motor Company and many other manufacturers that once followed this approach have since adopted the new way of organizing work, which features more employee empowerment.

As you read this selection, keep in mind that you are "listening" to the voice of a man who is revealing his personal feelings about a job situation that often ignores such feelings.

On a separate sheet of paper, draw a line down the center to make two columns. In the left-hand column, note words and phrases that Phil Stallings uses to describe what it is like to work on the assembly line and how he and other workers feel about their jobs—phrases such as "the noise, oh it's tremendous" and "some guys are uptight." In the right-hand column, note your reactions to these words and phrases.

Meet Studs Terkel

The writing of Studs Terkel owes a lot to the tape recorder. He has traveled all over the country, tape recorder in hand, interviewing people from all levels of society. Some of his interviews are with celebrities, but his most interesting ones are with "real people," ordinary citizens who open up and talk about their work, their families, their hopes and fears. "I celebrate the non-celebrated," he once said.

Terkel's first name is actually Louis. He took the name "Studs" from a fictional character, Studs Lonigan, who appears in several novels written by James T. Farrell during the 1930s.

Terkel was born in 1912 in New York City. After earning his bachelor's and law degrees at the University of Chicago, he worked as a civil-service employee in Washington, D.C., then as a stage actor, movie-house manager, radio and television broadcaster, and writer.

One of his books, *"The Good War": An Oral History of World War II,* won the Pulitzer Prize in 1985. Terkel said he used the phrase "The Good War" to drive home the irony of any war's being good. Among his other works are *Giants of Jazz*; *Hard Times: An Oral History of the Great Depression; American Dreams: Lost and Found,* all non-fiction; and *Amazing Grace,* a play.

Bill Burke, Archive (Courtesy *Esquire* magazine)

spot-welder—a worker who stands in one spot on an assembly line and joins metallic parts by heating them with a welding machine

Phil Stallings

He is a spot-welder at the Ford assembly plant on the far South Side of Chicago. He is twenty-seven years old; recently married. He works the third shift: 3:30 P.M. to midnight.

"I start the automobile, the first welds. From there it goes to another line, where the floor's put on, the roof, the trunk hood, the doors. Then it's put on a frame. There is hundreds of lines.

"The welding gun's got a square handle, with a button on the top for high voltage and a button on the bottom for low. The first is to clamp the metal together. The second is to fuse it.

"The gun hangs from a ceiling, over tables that ride on a track. It travels in a circle, oblong, like an egg. You stand on a cement platform, maybe six inches from the ground."

I stand in one spot, about two- or three-feet area, all night. The only time a person stops is when the line stops. We do about thirty-two jobs per car, per unit. Forty-eight units an hour, eight hours a day. Thirty-two times forty-eight times eight. Figure it out. That's how many times I push that button.

The noise, oh it's tremendous. You open your mouth and you're liable to get a mouthful of sparks.

The noise, oh it's tremendous. You open your mouth and you're liable to get a mouthful of sparks. (Shows his arms) That's a burn, these are burns. You don't compete against the noise. You go to yell and at the same time you're straining to maneuver the gun to where you have to weld.

You got some guys that are uptight, and they're not sociable. It's too rough. You pretty much stay to yourself. You get involved with yourself. You dream, you think of things you've done. I drift back continuously to when I was a kid and what me and my brothers did. The things you love most are the things you drift back into.

Lots of times I worked from the time I started to the time

"Phil Stallings" from _Working_ by Studs Terkel. ©1972 by Studs Terkel. Reprinted by permission of Pantheon Books, a division of Random House, Inc.

of the break and I never realized I had even worked. When you dream, you reduce the chances of friction with the foreman or with the next guy.

It don't stop. It just goes and goes and goes. I bet there's men who have lived and died out there, never seen the end of that line. And they never will—because it's endless. It's like a serpent. It's just all body, no tail. It can do things to you…(Laughs.)

Repetition is such that if you were to think about the job itself, you'd slowly go out of your mind.

Repetition is such that if you were to think about the job itself, you'd slowly go out of your mind. You'd let your problems build up, you'd get to a point where you'd be at the fellow next to you—his throat. Every time the foreman came by and looked at you, you'd have something to say. You just strike out at anything you can. So if you involve yourself by yourself, you overcome this.

I don't like the pressure, the intimidation. How would you like to go up to someone and say, "I would like to go to the bathroom?" If the foreman doesn't like you, he'll make you hold it, just ignore you. Should I leave this job to go to the bathroom I risk being fired. The line moves all the time.

I work next to Jim Grayson and he's preoccupied. The guy on my left, he's a Mexican, speaking Spanish, so it's pretty hard to understand him. You just avoid him. Brophy, he's a young fella, he's going to college. He works catty-corner from me. Him and I talk from time to time. If he ain't in the mood, I don't talk. If I ain't in the mood, he knows it.

Oh sure, there's tension here. It's not always obvious, but the whites stay with the whites and the coloreds stay with the coloreds. When you go into Ford, Ford says, "Can you work with other men?" This stops a lot of trouble, 'cause when you're working side by side with a guy, they can't afford to have guys fighting. When two men don't socialize, that means two guys are gonna do more work, know what I mean?

I don't understand how come more guys don't flip. Because you're nothing more than a machine when you hit this type of thing. They give better care to that machine than they will to you. They'll have more respect, give more attention to that machine. And you *know* this. Somehow you get the feeling that the machine is better than you are. (Laughs.)

intimidation—the act of frightening or threatening someone

preoccupied—lost in thought; having your mind focused on one thing instead of another

catty-corner—on a diagonal line (for example, "The house stood catty-corner to the store across the intersection.")

109

Brenda Grannan

XL—a model of Ford automobile

You really begin to wonder. What price do they put on me? Look at the price they put on the machine. If that machine breaks down, there's somebody out there to fix it right away. If I break down, I'm just pushed over to the other side till another man takes my place. The only thing they have on their mind is to keep that line running.

I'll do the best I can. I believe in an eight-hour pay for an eight-hour day. But I will not try to out-reach my limits. If I can't cut it, I just don't do it. I've been there three years and I keep my nose pretty clean. I never cussed anybody or anything like that. But I've had some real brushes with foremen.

What happened was my job was overloaded. I got cut and it got infected. I got blood poisoning. The drill broke. I took it to the foreman's desk. I says, "Change this as soon as you can." We were running specials for XL hoods. I told him I wasn't a repair man. That's how the conflict began. I says, "If you want, take me to the Green House." Which is a superintendent's office—disciplinary station. This is when he says, "Guys like you I'd like to see in the parking lot."

One foreman I know, he's about the youngest out here, he has this idea: I'm it and if you don't like it, you know what you can do. Anything this other foreman says, he usually overrides. Even in some cases, the foremen don't get along. They're pretty hard to live with, even with each other.

Oh yeah, the foreman's got somebody knuckling down on him, putting the screws to him. But a foreman is still free to go to the bathroom, go get a cup of coffee. He doesn't face the penalties. When I first went in there, I kind of envied foremen. Now, I wouldn't have a foreman's job. I wouldn't give 'em the time of the day.

When a man becomes a foreman, he has to forget about even being human, as far as feelings are concerned. You see a guy there bleeding to death. So what, buddy? That line's gotta keep goin'. I can't live like that. To me, if a man gets hurt, first thing you do is get him some attention.

About the blood poisoning. It came from the inside of a hood rubbin' against me. It caused quite a bit of pain. I went down to the medics. They said it was a boil. Got to my doctor that night. He said blood poisoning. Running fever and all this. Now I've smartened up.

They have a department of medics. It's basically first aid. There's no doctor on our shift, just two or three nurses, that's it. They've got a door with a sign on it that says Lab. Another door with a sign on it: Major Surgery. But my own personal opinion, I'm afraid of 'em. I'm afraid if I were to get hurt, I'd get nothin' but back talk. I got hit square in the chest one day with a bar from a rack and it cut me down this side. They didn't take x-rays or nothing. Sent me back on the job. I missed three and a half days two weeks ago. I had bronchitis. They told me I was all right. I didn't have a fever. I went home and my doctor told me I couldn't go back to work for two weeks. I really needed the money, so I had to go back the next day. I woke up still sick, so I took off the rest of the week.

I pulled a muscle on my neck, straining. This gun, when you grab this thing from the ceiling, cable, weight, I mean you're pulling everything. Your neck, your shoulders, and your back. I'm very surprised more accidents don't happen. You have to lean over, at the same time holding down the gun. This whole edge here is sharp. I go through a shirt every two weeks, it just goes right through. My coveralls catch on fire. I've had gloves catch on fire. (Indicates arms) See them little holes? That's what sparks do. I've got burns across here from last night.

I'll work like a dog until I get what I want.

I know I could find better places to work. But where could I get the money I'm making? Let's face it, $4.32 an hour. That's real good money now. Funny thing is, I don't mind working at body construction. To a great degree, I enjoy it. I love using my hands—more than I do my mind. I love to be able to put things together and see something in the long run. I'll be the first to admit I've got the easiest job on the line. But I'm against this thing where I'm being held back. I'll work like a dog until I get what I want. The job I really want is utility.

It's where I can stand and say I can do any job in this department, and nobody has to worry about me. As it is now, out of say, sixty jobs, I can do almost half of 'em. I want to get away from standing in one spot. Utility can do a different job every day. Instead of working right there for eight hours I could work over there for eight, I could work the other place for eight. Every day it would change. I would be around more people. I go out on my lunch break and work on the fork truck

bronchitis—a disease of the lungs

111

for a half-hour—to get the experience. As soon as I got it down pretty good, the foreman in charge says he'll take me. I don't want the other guys to see me. When I hit that fork lift, you just stop your thinking and you concentrate. Something right there in front of you, not in the past, not in the future. This is real healthy.

I don't eat lunch at work. I may grab a candy bar, that's enough. I wouldn't be able to hold it down. The tension your body is put under by the speed of the line...When you hit them brakes, you just can't stop. There's a certain momentum that carries you forward. I could hold the food, but it wouldn't set right.

Proud of my work? How can I feel pride in a job where I call a foreman's attention to a mistake, a bad piece of equipment, and he'll ignore it. Pretty soon you get the idea they don't care. You keep doing this and finally you're titled a troublemaker. So you just go about your work. You *have* to have pride. So you throw it off to something else. And that's my stamp collection.

I'd break both my legs to get into social work. I see all over so many kids really gettin' a raw deal. I think I'd go into juvenile. I tell kids on the line, "Man, go out there and get that college." Because it's too late for me now.

When you go into Ford, first thing they try to do is break your spirit. I seen them bring a tall guy where they needed a short guy. I seen them bring a short guy where you have to stand on two guys' backs to do something. Last night, they brought a fifty-eight-year-old man to do the job I was on. That man's my father's age. I know damn well my father couldn't do it. To me, this is humanely wrong. A job should be a job, not a death sentence.

I go out on my lunch break and work on the fork truck...to get the experience.

The younger worker, when he gets uptight, he talks back. But you take an old fellow, he's got a year, two years, maybe three years to go. If it was me, I wouldn't say a word, I wouldn't care what they did. 'Cause, baby, for another two years I can stick it out. I can't blame this man. I respect him because he had enough will power to stick it out for thirty years.

It's gonna change. There's a trend. We're getting younger and younger men. We got this new Thirty and Out. Thirty years seniority and out. The whole idea is to give a man more time, more time to slow down and live. While he's still in his fifties, he can settle down in a camper and go out and fish. I've sat down and thought about it. I've got twenty-seven years to go. (Laughs.) That's why I don't go around causin' trouble or lookin' for a cause.

The only time I get involved is when it affects me or it affects a man on the line in a condition that could be me. I don't believe in lost causes, but when it all happened…(He pauses, appears bewildered.)

The whole idea is to give a man more time, more time to slow down and live.

The foreman was riding the guy. The guy either told him to go away or pushed him, grabbed him…You can't blame the guy—Jim Grayson. I don't want nobody stickin' their finger in my face. I'd've probably hit him beside the head. The whole thing was: Damn it, it's about time we took a stand. Let's stick up for the guy. We stopped the line. (He pauses, grins.) Ford lost about twenty units. I'd figure about five grand a unit—whattaya got? (Laughs.)

I said, "Let's all go home." When the line's down like that, you can go up to one man and say, "You gonna work?" If he says no, they can fire him. See what I mean? But if nobody was there, who the hell were they gonna walk up to and say, "Are you gonna work?" Man, there woulda been nobody there! If it were up to me, we'd gone home.

Jim Grayson, the guy I work next to, he's colored. Absolutely. That's the first time I've seen unity on that line. Now it's happened once, it'll happen again. Because everybody just sat down. Believe you me. (Laughs.) It stopped at eight and it didn't start till twenty after eight. Everybody and his brother were down there. It was really nice to see, it really was.

Trying It Out

Responding to "Phil Stallings"

Now that you have read the literature selection, answer the following questions. Whenever possible, use evidence from the article to support your answers.

1 Review the words or phrases that you wrote down while reading the article. Do they have a common theme? If so, what is it? What is your reaction to these words and phrases?

2 Review the words or phrases that you and your classmates compiled at the beginning of this lesson about your own experiences with repetitive work. How do they compare with the words and phrases used by Phil Stallings? What are the similarities and differences between your experiences and those that Stallings describes?

3 How are Phil Stallings's feelings affected by his supervisors' actions?

4 What are the tensions he feels? How does he manage to survive in this work environment?

5 How do you think Stallings would respond to working for a company where employees were empowered and were asked to anticipate problems and solve them creatively? That kind of workplace was described in Lesson 2.

Be prepared to share your answers with the class.

"Workplace illnesses associated with stresses from repeated motions of wrists and limbs... now make up more than three-fifths of all occupational illnesses recorded by employers. In 1983 there were about 27,000 recorded cases of repetitive motion disorder. In 1991 nearly 224,000 repetitive motion disorder cases were reported by the Bureau of Labor Statistics."

—Robert B. Reich,
Secretary of Labor, U.S. Department of Labor

Interviewing a Classmate

Think about the role Studs Terkel played in creating this literature selection. Although the words belong to Phil Stallings, it was Terkel who interviewed him and made him feel comfortable enough to talk about personal matters. And it was Terkel who wrote up the interview in the form that you read.

Imagine that you are Studs Terkel. Interview a student in your class to find out about his or her work situation (in school or at a job). Before you do the interview, generate a list of four or five questions to ask this student—questions such as these:

What is a typical workday like for you? How do you feel about your work environment? What are the physical conditions? What are the mental conditions?

As you conduct the interview, keep in mind that a good interviewer will

- listen carefully to the interviewee's responses.

- take careful notes on what the interviewee says.

- make an effort to draw out the interviewee's true feelings.

When you finish your interview, switch roles and respond to the other student's questions.

> ### Why Do Horses Like Machines?
>
> During the past 150 years, machines have made life easier not only for people but also for work animals.
>
> In 1850 animals performed an estimated 52 percent of all work in the United States. People did 13 percent, and machines were used for 35 percent.
>
> Today, however, machines do more than 98 percent of our work, people do only one percent, and animals do less than one percent.

Summing Up

Writing up the Interview

Use your notes to write up the interview you conducted with your classmate. Follow Studs Terkel's format, presenting it as a first-person statement by the student you interviewed. Try to use the interviewee's exact words, as much as possible. If desired, you may change the interviewee's name.

Be prepared to share and discuss your written interview with the class. Compare your interviewee's situation and feelings with those of Phil Stallings. How do the words or phrases used in your interview resemble or differ from those in Terkel's interview?

Finally, discuss the interviewing and the interview-writing processes. Were they easy or difficult? What did you like or dislike about doing them?

115

Keeping Track

On a separate sheet of paper, answer the following questions. Use what you have learned in this lesson to help you.

1 Why are conditions often stressful for employees in the industrial workplace?

2 What effect can these stressful conditions have on relations between supervisors and workers?

3 How do some workers manage to survive these stressful working conditions?

Going Further

■ Expand your interviewing skills and learn more about an actual occupational area. Either individually or in a small group, obtain permission to interview a worker from a local business place or manufacturing plant. Arrange to conduct the interview at a time that is convenient for the worker. Jot down a list of questions that are similar to the ones you used in this lesson to interview a classmate. Spend some time practicing your questions with another student. When you meet with the worker, begin by learning something about the job situation, then conduct the interview. Explain to the employee that his or her responses will be used only for this class and that the worker may remain anonymous. Write up the interview in a way that gives a clear picture of how the worker feels about the job situation. Be prepared to share your written interview with the class.

■ Imagine that you have the money to start a new company. You are in a position to create the company's work environment in any way you choose. On a separate piece of paper, describe in general terms the kind of company you would start and the work environment you would create. Then explain how this environment compares with the assembly plant where Phil Stallings works. Be prepared to share your paper with the class.

Looking for a Job? The "Big Three" Are Hiring

University of Michigan auto researcher Sean McAlinden says the Big Three [Ford, Chrysler, and General Motors] will need to hire up to 200,000 hourly workers by the end of the decade to replace retiring employees. Roughly 90,000 of those jobs will be in Michigan. "We've been calling it the great turnover," McAlinden said. "This is a rate of attrition that hasn't been matched in the auto industry since the Great Depression."

—Rick Haglund, "Retirements Mean Big 3 Will Be Hiring," *Ann Arbor News* (May 1, 1994)

Applying What You Have Learned

An Application Lesson with Video

Looking Ahead

What This Lesson Is About

In this lesson, you will use what you have learned in this module to help you create written instructions for workers in a vocational area that interests you.

✔ Wherever you work, effective communication skills are critical to your relationships with co-workers and supervisors.

✔ Safety is an important consideration in the workplace, and employers must communicate safety instructions to their workers.

✔ You can use your communication skills to create written safety instructions for new workers in a workplace situation.

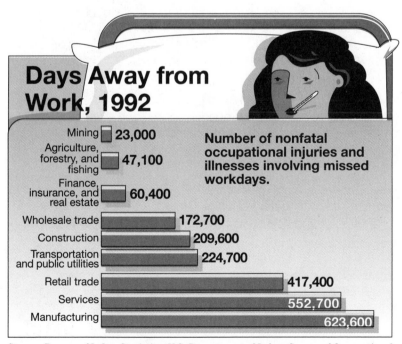

Days Away from Work, 1992

Number of nonfatal occupational injuries and illnesses involving missed workdays.

Mining	23,000
Agriculture, forestry, and fishing	47,100
Finance, insurance, and real estate	60,400
Wholesale trade	172,700
Construction	209,600
Transportation and public utilities	224,700
Retail trade	417,400
Services	552,700
Manufacturing	623,600

Source: Bureau of Labor Statistics, U.S. Department of Labor, Survey of Occupational Injuries and Illnesses

117

Key Ideas

athletic trainer—a professional person who guides the training activities of athletes

physical therapist—a professional person who treats disease by physical and mechanical means, such as exercise and massage

safety—the state of being free from the risk of experiencing or causing danger or injury

Viewing the Videodisc— Rebound Sports Medicine

You are about to view a videodisc or videocassette segment about physicians, physical therapists, and athletic trainers who work as a team to treat persons with injuries sustained while playing sports.

As you watch the segment, ask yourself,

"How do these medical professionals achieve and maintain an effective working relationship?"

Rebound Sports Medicine

Search 22292, Play To 29439

Company Profile

Company Name: Rebound Sports Medicine Centers

Location: Bloomington, Indiana

Mission Statement: Rebound Sports Medicine Centers are dedicated to providing high-quality and affordable patient care for orthopedic, performance, and industrial injuries. Rebound is committed to increasing community awareness of Bloomington Hospital and its services through educational programs and involvement in special community events.

Company Products and/or Services: "We are a resource for orthopedic and athletic injuries. Once a patient has been evaluated by a physician, we are a care provider for physical therapy and athletic training services necessitated by orthopedic, sports, and work-related injuries. We also offer internship and volunteer programs for students of physical therapy and athletic training, as well as for those in other health fields. We provide coverage for community athletic events. We can also provide educational clinics on various topics."

Clients and Customers: Patients come from a six-county area in southern Indiana. Typical problems include foot, ankle, shoulder, back, and neck injuries. Other clients include universities, businesses, government agencies, high schools, junior highs, and elementary schools.

Number of Employees: 20

Unique Features: "We offer a combination of two services: physical therapy and athletic training. Some members of our staff have dual credentials. We serve traditional athletes, "industrial athletes" (employees in the workplace), and performing artists. Our specialty is treating persons with general orthopedic injuries."

118

Post-Viewing Questions

After you have watched the video segment, respond to the following:

1 The Rebound crew working the basketball tourney takes "a team approach to the patient." What role does communication play in this approach? Give examples.

2 The team includes persons with different training (physical therapists, athletic trainers, doctors). How does this affect communication?

3 At the basketball tourney, what are some barriers that might affect communication among Rebound team members?

Be prepared to share your answers with the class.

Rebound Sports Medicine:
Discussion Question 1

Search Frame 29440

Rebound Sports Medicine:
Discussion Question 2

Search Frame 29441

Rebound Sports Medicine:
Discussion Question 3

Search Frame 29442

> *"At the Gus Macker tourney, good communication can make the difference between winning and losing. And the same thing is true for the Rebound team, where co-workers with different experiences and skills somehow make it all look easy."*

Getting Started

Worker Safety

Safety is an important consideration in all workplaces. This is clearly true for workers in a medical setting, such as the Rebound team you saw in the video segment. Safety is even an issue for workers at computer terminals, for they may be affected by electromagnetic forces or by the pain of doing repetitive tasks.

Many businesses and industries try to lessen the chance of injury and death and to cut the cost of damage claims by issuing safety regulations for their workers to follow. For example, Rebound team members follow careful procedures to protect themselves from infection while they perform their duties.

Employers often create written safety instructions that are distributed to workers or posted prominently in the workplace. Such instructions can take many forms.

119

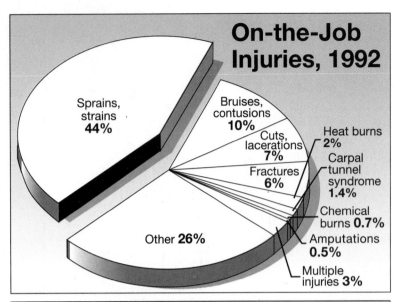

On-the-Job Injuries, 1992

Sprains, strains **44%**

Bruises, contusions **10%**

Cuts, lacerations **7%**

Fractures **6%**

Heat burns **2%**

Carpal tunnel syndrome **1.4%**

Chemical burns **0.7%**

Amputations **0.5%**

Multiple injuries **3%**

Other **26%**

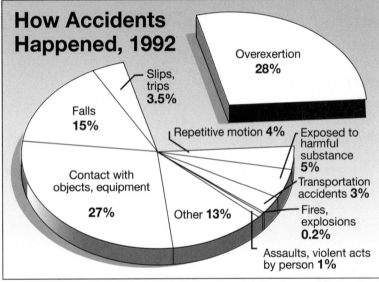

How Accidents Happened, 1992

Overexertion **28%**

Slips, trips **3.5%**

Falls **15%**

Repetitive motion **4%**

Exposed to harmful substance **5%**

Transportation accidents **3%**

Contact with objects, equipment **27%**

Other **13%**

Fires, explosions **0.2%**

Assaults, violent acts by person **1%**

Source: Bureau of Labor Statistics, U.S. Department of Labor, Survey of Occupational Injuries and Illnesses

Some safety instructions list procedures to follow in case of an accident or fire in the workplace. Others tell workers the proper ways to guard their machinery or to handle hazardous materials. In eating places, employees are expected to follow sanitary procedures. Truck and taxi drivers receive instructions on safe driving. Farm workers and lawn-care specialists receive instructions on the use of insecticides, herbicides, and fertilizers. Office workers may have rules to follow for the safe use of computer terminals. Miners must follow safety regulations when they work in the mines.

Whatever the nature of the workplace, written safety instructions follow the rules you learned in Lesson 6 for giving written directions. But since safety instructions can be a matter of life or death, you want them to be especially simple and clear.

On the basis of what you have just read, answer the following questions:

1 Why are safety instructions so important in the workplace?

2 What are some examples of safety instructions for workers?

3 What do you remember about the rules for writing instructions that you learned in Lesson 6?

4 Why must all safety instructions be written simply and clearly?

Be prepared to share your answers with the class.

Trying It Out

Writing Safety Instructions for Workers in Your Vocational Field

In Lesson 6, you created instructions for dishwashers. Now you can try your hand at creating safety instructions for new workers in a vocational field that interests you. These instructions will tell new workers exactly how to perform a task or tasks in as safe a manner as possible. Follow these steps:

1 Form a group with other students who are interested in your occupational area.

2 Review Lesson 6, "Following and Giving Written Instructions." In that lesson, you learned how to write instructions. You also made a job aid, an outline of the seven steps for writing instructions. Review the instruction-writing procedure. When you get to step 5, be sure to review the four substeps that deal with the actual writing of instructions.

3 Decide on a particular type of worker (in the occupational field you have selected) who will receive your written instructions. Also decide what topic your instructions will cover. Some suggestions appear below. You may wish to choose one of them; or, if your instructor approves, devise your own topic.

If your occupational area is:	…you may choose to write safety instructions for a new employee to:
Agriculture/ natural resources	• treat lawns for weed pests • treat crops for insect pests • prevent forest fires • treat poisonous snakebites
Mechanics/ transportation	• change an auto battery • drive trucks long distances • handle an airliner emergency • transport hazardous materials • deliver newspapers by bicycle
Business and computer technologies	• use a computer terminal • exit a building in case of fire • drive a company or rented car • travel to foreign countries
Health and human services	• handle violent persons • treat a patient with oxygen • prevent worker infections • care for preschool-age children • prepare food
Engineering technologies	• work on power lines • survey streets and highways • inspect elevators • install electrical systems
Construction and design	• do roofing • work on a tall building • operate heavy equipment • bring visitors to a construction site
Communication technologies	• install cable or satellite systems • film events in a hazardous area • contain crows at a music concert

Remember, Lift with Your Legs

Of the 80 million Americans who suffer from chronic back pain each year, four out of five cases could have been prevented. Back problems are the most common work injury today, usually striking people between the ages of 20 and 50. According to *The Power of Pain* by Shirly Kraus, 100 million Americans are either permanently disabled or are less productive due to back pain. And those who work lose about five workdays per year, a productivity loss of $55 billion.

—James A. Traficant, Jr., "Health Care Reform," *Congressional Record* (Feb. 2, 1994)

121

4 Do research to learn which points your instructions should cover. Go to the school or public library to find books, articles, or government publications that tell about safety regulations for the topic you have chosen. Many federal, state, and local agencies deal with safety matters, and many of them issue reports and regulations. The Federal Aviation Administration handles air travel. The Environmental Protection Agency regulates toxic chemicals and environmental hazards. The Occupational Safety and Health Review Commission oversees workplace safety. Highway safety is the concern of both the Federal Highway Administration and the National Highway Traffic Safety Administration, while the National Transportation Safety Board deals with safety problems in all types of transportation. The Mine Safety and Health Administration regulates mines, and the Food Safety and Inspection Service inspects meat and poultry products. Your state and local fire departments issue fire regulations, and your city or county building department oversees building codes.

5 Visit a local workplace that operates in your chosen vocational area. Interview administrators, managers, or workers about safety regulations. Find out what topics need to be addressed in issuing safety instructions to a new employee in a real-world workplace.

6 On the basis of your library research and your interviews, create your instructions. Follow the suggestions for good writing that you learned in Lesson 6 and reviewed in this lesson. Keep in mind that you are writing instructions involving safety and that these instructions are for a new worker; therefore, make your instructions simple, straightforward, and complete.

Summing Up

Checking It Out

After you have written your safety instructions, exchange your work with that of another group. Use a copy of the **Safety Instructions Feedback** form to provide feedback on their work, while they supply feedback on yours. See how well their safety instructions meet the criteria for giving effective written instructions. They will do the same for you.

Based on the feedback you receive, revise your safety instructions as necessary. Keep a copy of your instructions in your portfolio.

Safety Instructions Feedback

Audience and Purpose

_____ Do the instructions tell the new co-workers what they need to know?

_____ Is the language appropriate for the co-workers' level of understanding?

_____ Do the instructions identify and fulfill their purpose?

Content

_____ Do the instructions give all the necessary directions?

_____ Is the information given correctly?

_____ Is the information given simply and briefly?

_____ Is there any unnecessary information?

Organization

_____ Are any elements missing?

_____ Are the instructions arranged in the correct order?

_____ If a summary diagram would help, is one included?

Design

_____ Is the design appropriate for a list of instructions?

_____ Are the most important words or sentences emphasized appropriately?

_____ Are headings used effectively?

_____ Are useful illustrations included?

Clarity

_____ Is the wording clear?

_____ Is the wording accurate?

_____ Is the wording consistent?

_____ Does each instruction begin with an action word?

_____ Are there any unnecessary words?

_____ Did a co-worker test the instructions and find them usable?

Grammar, Spelling, and Punctuation

_____ Is the writing grammatically correct?

_____ Are there any errors in spelling or punctuation?

Going Further

- Workplaces of the industrial age were often very dangerous places. Neither employers nor employees took many safety precautions, and as a result, the death and injury rate among workers was high. The movement for worker safety is largely a product of the 20th century. In your school or public library, find books and articles that tell how the safety movement developed in the United States. Write a few paragraphs reporting what you learn. Be prepared to share your findings with the class.

Sleep Stats

220,000
Average hours in a lifetime spent sleeping.

15%
The approximate number of adults in the U.S. and Canada who say they're drowsy on any given day.

$70,000,000,000
The estimated cost to businesses in lost productivity, industrial accidents and higher medical bills due to disrupted sleep and sleep disorders.

Source: The Better Sleep Council/Graphic by Brenda Grannan, *The Cincinnati Enquirer*

- Although the term "physical therapy" was not coined until 1922, the use of physical means such as exercise and massage for treating disease probably goes back to the Stone Age. In the library, find books and articles on physical therapy (or physiotherapy). Read them to find out how this type of therapy helps patients with joint and muscular diseases. Also interview a physical therapist about this form of treatment. Write a short essay on what you discover. Be prepared to share your essay with your classmates.

- Write a brief essay about ways this module has helped you improve your communication skills. Be prepared to share your essay with the class.

Teens Pick Top 10 Careers

According to a survey of teenagers by *Careers & Colleges* magazine, physical therapy was the top career choice of the 4,900 teenagers who responded.

Other careers that made the "Top Ten" list include FBI agent, accountant, lawyer, architect, veterinarian, environmental engineer, psychotherapist, business manager, and pharmacist, in that order.

Appendix

Glossary

active voice—a sentence structure that emphasizes the actor ("Tiffany threw the ball.")

alliteration—the repetition of consonant sounds that begin words, for example "wet, windy weekend"

appeal—an urgent request or persuasive message; an earnest plea for assistance or cooperation

assertive—being disposed to state a position strongly or positively; bold; confident

athletic trainer—a professional person who guides the training activities of athletes

communication style—a person's customary way of relating to other persons

counterproductive—hindering the production of something; working against the attainment of a goal

creative—imaginative; being able to produce something or make something happen by using imaginative skills

dehumanizing—the kind of task that deprives a person of human qualities or individual personality

director—an energetic person whose emphasis is on task performance

downsizing—reduction in size of the work force, usually because of the loss of business income or a general downturn in the economy

electronic mail (e-mail)—written messages entered and instantly delivered through a computer network

electronic monitoring—the use of video cameras, computer systems, or telephone hookups to observe other persons, including employees in the workplace

employee empowerment—a management philosophy that gives employees more opportunities to generate new ideas, to solve problems, and to share in making decisions

etiquette—procedures prescribed to achieve smooth social relations

flame—to make inflammatory or hurtful statements in an e-mail message; a confrontational e-mail message

flowchart—a diagram showing the steps in an activity, process, or procedure

improvise—speaking or acting on the spur of the moment

jargon—specialized or technical language used in a particular trade or profession

job aid—a written checklist for a worker to follow in completing a task

job description—a statement of duties and desired performance levels for a specified position in the workplace

job sharing—having the same job and work space as another person but working at different times of the day

narrator—the person or character who tells a story or provides commentary on it

negotiation—a process for resolving differences and reaching agreement through discussion and bargaining

passive voice—a sentence structure that emphasizes the object of the action ("The ball was thrown by Tiffany.")

performance review or job evaluation—a formal process for determining an employee's progress

persuasive—believable and convincing

physical therapist—a professional person who treats disease by physical and mechanical means, such as exercise and massage

proactive—anticipating problems and taking forceful action to solve them or head them off

racist—having or expressing a racial or ethnic bias, fear, or prejudice

relater—a cautious person who emphasizes relations with others

sexist—having or expressing a bias, fear, or prejudice arising from differences in gender

socializer—an energetic person who emphasizes relations with others

surveillance—keeping a close watch over someone

target audience—the individuals you intend to reach with your message

thinker—a cautious person whose emphasis is on task performance

tone—a particular mood or attitude in writing or speech

worker productivity—amount of goods or services produced by an average worker in a specified amount of time

Additional Resources

Books and Articles

Axtell, Roger E., editor, *Do's and Taboos around the World* (New York: John Wiley & Sons, 1993).

Bower, Sharon Anthony, and Gordon H. Bower, *Asserting Yourself: A Practical Guide for Positive Change* (Reading, MA: Addison-Wesley Publishing, 1976).

Peters, Tom, *The Tom Peters Seminar: Crazy Times Call for Crazy Organizations* (New York: Vintage, 1994).

Tannen, Deborah, *Talking from 9 to 5* (New York: William Morrow, 1994).

Literature

Asimov, Isaac, *I, Robot* (St. Albans, VT: Panther, 1973).

> The work done by robots in a futuristic society serves as a metaphor for the evolution of human communication, especially among co-workers.

Coleman, John R., "From Man to Boy" in *The Art of Work: An Anthology of Workplace Literature* by James Coughlin and Christine B. LaRocco (Cincinnati: South-Western Educational Publishing, 1996).

> Coleman's journal entry discusses his being called "boy" at one of his earliest jobs, and it examines people's lack of respect for workers in certain positions.

Dana, Henry, *Two Years before the Mast* (New York: Buccaneer Books, 1981).

> This realistic account illustrates the importance of effective communication among co-workers on a merchant ship.

Howe, Louise Kapp, *Pink Collar Workers: Inside the World of Women's Work* (New York: Avon Books, 1977).

> Women discuss their job expectations and their communication with supervisors, co-workers, and clients.

Narayan, R.K, "45 a Month" in *The Art of Work: An Anthology of Workplace Literature* by James Coughlin and Christine B. LaRocco (Cincinnati: South-Western Educational Publishing, 1996).

> Shanta's father has promised to take her to the movies, but his boss won't let him leave work on time. He plans to quit his job, but instead he gets a raise and has to disappoint his daughter.

Selldon, Bernice, *The Mill Girls: Lucy Larcom, Harriet Hanson Robinson, and Sarah Bagley* (New York: Macmillan, 1983).

> Women discuss their experiences in the cotton mills and tell how they communicated with their supervisors.

Sinclair, Upton, *The Jungle* (Toronto: Bantam, 1981).

> This work focuses on the abuse of workers in the meat-packing industry in Chicago and the struggle of organized labor.

Sproul, Robert C., *Stronger than Steel: The Wayne Alderson Story* (San Francisco: Harper San Francisco, 1983).

> Vignettes about the Pittsburgh steel mills describe tough union members working together to solve problems.

Video

We strongly suggest you preview all videos.

Catch-22 directed by Mike Nichols, based on Joseph Heller's novel (Hollywood: Paramount, 1970). (2:01)

> A superior makes it difficult for an officer to obtain a discharge from the army.

Of Mice and Men directed by Gary Sinise, based on John Steinbeck's novel (Los Angeles: MGM/UA, 1992). (1:50)

> Two co-workers dream of a time when they can share the ownership of a rabbit farm in California.

Twelve Angry Men directed by Sidney Lumet, based on the play by Reginald Rose (Los Angeles: United Artists, 1957). (1:35)

> Twelve members of a jury express differing viewpoints as they debate a defendant's guilt or innocence.

On-line Services

On-line services can be used to enhance instruction and increase classroom resources. The five most popular commercial on-line services include

> **America Online** (800/827-6364), **CompuServe** (800/848-8199), **Delphi Internet Services Corporation** (800/695-4005), **GEnie Services** (800/638-9636), and **PRODIGY** (800-PRODIGY, 800/776-3449).

128

Acknowledgments

Literature Acknowledgments

Module 1—Védrine, Martha F. "Who Am I?" copyright ©1994 Martha Florence Védrine, from *In Our Own Words*, a special issue by and about urban youth. First published in the *Boston Globe Magazine*, February 6, 1994. • Gonzalez, Sheila. "Dear Dad," copyright ©1994 Sheila Gonzalez, from *In Our Own Words*, a special issue by and about urban youth. First published in the *Boston Globe Magazine*, February 6, 1994. • Gibson, William. Act III of *The Miracle Worker*, copyright ©1956, 1957 by William Gibson; copyright ©1959, 1969 by Tamarack Productions, Ltd., and George S. Kline and Leo Garel as trustees under three separate deeds of trust; renewed copyright ©1977 by William Gibson. Reprinted with permission of Atheneum Publishers, an imprint of Macmillan Publishing Company. No performance of any kind may be given without permission in writing from the author's agent, Samuel French, Inc., 45 W. 25th St., New York, NY 10010. • Bethancourt, T. Ernesto. "User Friendly," from *Connections: Short Stories*, edited by Donald R. Gallo; copyright ©1989 by T. Ernesto Bethancourt. Reprinted with permission of Delacorte Press, a division of Bantam Doubleday Dell Publishing Group, Inc. **Module 2**—Nolan, Christopher. Selections from *Under the Eye of the Clock: The Life Story of Christopher Nolan*, copyright ©1987. Reprinted with permission of George Weidenfeld & Nicholson, Ltd. • Martin, Molly. "Sweetheart," from *Tradeswomen* Magazine; later published in *If I Had a Hammer...* copyright ©1990. Reprinted with permission of the author. • McCullers, Carson. "Sucker," from *The Mortgaged Heart* by Carson McCullers; copyright ©1940, 1941, 1942, 1945, 1949, 1953, 1956, 1959, 1963, 1967, 1971 by Floria V. Lasky, executrix of the estate of Carson McCullers. Reprinted with permission of Houghton Mifflin Co. All rights reserved. **Module 3**—Hughes, Langston. "Theme for English B," copyright ©1951 by Langston Hughes; renewed copyright ©1979 by George Houston Bass. Reprinted with permission of Harold Ober Associates, Inc. • Macrorie, Ken. "World's Best Directions Writer," originally published in *College English* 15:5 by the National Council of Teachers of English. Public domain. • Hoey, Edwin. "Foul Shot," copyright ©1962, 1990 by Weekly Reader Corporation. Reprinted with permission of *Read* magazine, published by Weekly Reader Corporation. • Bischoff, John. "Bird on Basketball: How-to Strategies from the Great Celtics Champion," by Larry Bird with John Bischoff; copyright ©1983, 1985, 1986. Originally published in 1983 as "Larry Bird's Basketball: Birdwise" (Terre Haute, IN: Phoenix Projects). Reprinted with permission of the copyright owner/agent, W.W. Marketing, Inc., Jerry Wraley. **Module 4**—Roueché, Berton. "A Small, Apprehensive Child," copyright ©1984 by Berton Roueché. Reprinted with permission of Harold Ober Associates, Inc. • Burns, Christopher. "Three Mile Island: The Information Meltdown," from *Great Information Disasters*, compiled by Horton and Lewis (London: Aslib, copyright ©1991). **Module 5**—Walker,

Alice. "Expect Nothing," from *Revolutionary Petunias & Other Poems*, copyright ©1972 by Alice Walker. Reprinted with permission of Harcourt Brace & Co. • Clayton, Bernard, Jr. "How to Prepare the Six Vegetables Most Important to Stocks, Soups and Stews," "Le Minestrone," and "Cincinnati Chili," from *The Complete Book of Soups and Stews*, published by Simon and Schuster; copyright ©1984 by Bernard Clayton, Jr. Reprinted with permission of the author. • Malcolm X. Selection from *The Autobiography of Malcolm X*, written with the assistance of Alex Haley; copyright ©1964 by Alex Haley and Malcolm X and copyright ©1965 by Alex Haley and Betty Shabazz. Reprinted with permission of the publisher, Random House, Inc. **Module 6**—Zola, Meguido and Melanie. "Terry Fox," from the abridged version in the Gage Publishing Co. book *Connections 1*, (Picture-Life Series). Reprinted with permission of Grolier, Ltd., Toronto; copyright ©1984, 1990 by Grolier Ltd. • White, Bailey. "Fireman for Life," from *Mama Makes Up Her Mind and Other Dangers of Southern Living*, copyright ©1993 by Bailey White. Published by Addison-Wesley Publishing Co., Reading, MA. • Ellison, Harlan. " 'Repent, Harlequin!' Said the Ticktockman," copyright ©1965, 1993 by the author. Reprinted by arrangement with, and permission of, the author and his agent, Richard Curtis Associates, Inc., New York. All rights reserved. **Module 7**—Walker, Alice. "Everday Use," from *In Love and Trouble: Stories of Black Women*, copyright ©1973 by Alice Walker. Reprinted with permission of Harcourt Brace & Co. • Candelaria, Nash. "El Patrón," from *The Day the Cisco Kid Shot John Wayne* (1988). Reprinted with permission of Bilingual Press. • Reeves, Melanie. "A play: Boxing with Mom," copyright ©1994 Melanie Reeves, from *In Our Own Words*, a special issue by and about urban youth. First published in the *Boston Globe Magazine*, February 6, 1994. **Module 8**—Newman, Leslea. "Shifting Piles," from "Adjustments" in *Love Me Like You Mean It*, copyright ©1987, 1993 by Leslea Newman. Published by Clothespin Fever Press. Reprinted with permission of the author. • King, Martin Luther, Jr. Selected portions from "I Have a Dream," a speech delivered August 28, 1963, during the march for civil rights in Washington, DC.; copyright ©1963 by Martin Luther King, Jr.; renewed copyright ©1991 by Coretta Scott King. Reprinted by arrangement with the heirs to the estate of Martin Luther King, Jr., c/o Joan Daves Agency as agent for the proprietor. • Terkel, Studs. "Phil Stallings," from *Working*, copyright ©1972 by Studs Terkel. Reprinted with permission of Pantheon Books, a division of Random House, Inc. **Module 9**—Soto, Gary. "Oranges," from *New and Selected Poems*, copyright ©1995. Published by Chronicle Books. • Forbes, Kathryn. "Mama in the Hospital," from *Mama's Bank Account*, copyright ©1943 by Kathryn Forbes; renewed copyright ©1971 by Richard E. McLean and Robert M. McLean. Reprinted with permission of Harcourt Brace & Co. • Terkel, Studs. "Sharon Atkins," from *Working*, copyright ©1972 by Studs Terkel. Reprinted with permission of Pantheon Books,

Career Families:
What Kind of Career Do You Want?

Not sure? If you examine your interests and abilities, you may find career areas that are right for you. John Holland, a career development theorist, created a code that might help you explore career areas.

What is the Holland Code? In 1973, Dr. Holland created a system of breaking interests and abilities into six categories. He believed that every person fits into at least one category. Most people fit into two or three categories. Your personal combination of Holland categories is called your Holland Code.

What are the six categories? The six Holland categories, or families, are listed below. As you read the descriptions, try to decide which two or three families sound most like you.

- **Realistic.** These people have athletic or mechanical ability. They prefer to work with objects, machines, tools, plants, or animals. They usually like to work outdoors.

- **Investigative.** These are people who like to observe, learn, investigate, analyze, evaluate, or solve problems.

- **Artistic.** These people have artistic, innovative, or intuitive abilities. They usually like to work in an unstructured situation, using their imagination or creativity.

- **Social.** People in this category like to work with people. They like to inform, enlighten, help, train, develop, or cure people. They may also be skilled with words.

- **Enterprising.** These people also like to work with people, but they like to influence, persuade, or perform. They like to lead or manage for organizational goals or economic gain.

- **Conventional.** People in this group like to work with data, have clerical or numerical ability, and carry things out in detail. They usually enjoy following other people's instructions.

How do you figure out your Holland Code? Take the first letter of the three families that sound most like you, and put them in order of preference. For example, you may think Social (Holland Code S), Investigative (I), and Artistic (A) all sound like you. You then have to decide which of these three you prefer the most. Let's say it is Social. Then you need to decide whether you prefer Artistic or Investigative more. If it's Artistic, then Investigative, your Holland Code would be SAI.

What do you do now? You can use your Holland Code to match your interests and abilities to careers. Dr. Holland classified careers by how they fit the codes. Below are the six families and a *partial* listing of occupations that you may enjoy if you fall into that category. Do any of these careers interest you? Can you think of other careers that use the same kinds of interests and abilities?

- **Realistic.** Airplane Pilot, Carpenter, Civil Engineer, Drafter, Electrician, Forester, Mechanical Engineering Technician, Musical Instrument Tuner, Optician, Radio Operator.

- **Investigative.** Actuary, Agricultural Scientist, Computer Programmer, Economist, Medical Lab Assistant, Meteorologist, Physician, Radiologic Technologist, Tool and Die Maker, Speech Pathologist.

- **Artistic.** Advertising Agent, Architect, Archivist, Commercial Artist, Designer, Editor, Musician, Photolithographer, Public Relations Person, Technical Writer.

- **Social.** Building Manager, Clergy, College or University Administrator, Cosmetologist, Funeral Director, Health Administrator, Librarian, Personnel Director, Recreation Worker, Teacher.

131

- **Enterprising.** Florist, Food Service Manager, Lawyer, Military Attaché, Personnel Recruiter, Radio/TV Announcer, Real-estate Agent, Salesperson, Stockbroker, Surveyor.

- **Conventional.** Accountant, Bank Teller, Bookkeeper, Cashier, Credit Manager, Data Entry Keyer, General Office Worker, Insurance Claim Representative, Payroll Clerk, Reservations Agent.

How do I get more information? Get advice from your parents and friends. They may be able to help you decide which career families sound like you. You can also talk to your guidance counselor or a reference librarian. They may be able to help you get more information about the six career families or the Holland Code.

Remember, the Holland Code is not the only system to help you make career decisions. Many people created methods of career planning. There is no one right way to make decisions about your future. But it is important to consider the future…start now!

Careers: Which Ones Do You Want to Know More About?

Accountant and Auditor
Activities Therapist
Actor/Actress, Director, Producer
Actuary
Adult Vocational Education Teacher
Advertising Agent
Aerospace Engineer
Agricultural Engineer
Agricultural Scientist
Air-traffic Controller
Aircraft Mechanic
Airplane Pilot
Alarm System Installer and Repairer
Ambulance Attendant/Driver
Animal Caretaker
Apparel Workers
Architect
Archivist and Curator
Assembler (Precision)
Auto Body Repairer
Auto Mechanic
Auto Parts Service Clerk
Automobile Salesperson
Automobile Service Advisor
Bank Teller
Barber
Bartender
Bellhop/Bell Captain
Billing, Cost and Rate Clerks
Bindery Worker
Biological Scientist
Biomedical Engineer

Biomedical Equipment Technician
Blacksmith
Blue-collar Worker Supervisor
Boilermaker
Bookkeeper and Accounting Clerk
Brickmason/Stonemason
Broadcast Technician
Building Manager
Bulldozer Operator
Bus Driver
Carpenter
Carpet Installer
Cashier
Cement Mason and Terrazzo Worker
Ceramic Engineer
Chemical Engineer
Chemical Equipment Operator
Chemist
Child-care Worker
Chimney Sweep
Chiropractor
City Manager
Civil Engineer
Clergy
Clerical Supervisor
Clinical Laboratory Technologist
Collection Worker
College Faculty Member
Commercial Artist
Communication Equipment Mechanic
Compositor and Typesetter

Computer and Peripheral Equipment Operator
Computer Programmer
Computer Service Technician
Computer Systems Analyst
Construction and Building Inspector
Construction Laborer
Cook/Chef
Cooperative Extension Service Worker
Corrections Officer
Cosmetologist
Cost Estimator
Counselor
Counter and Rental Clerk
Court Administrator
Court Clerk
Court Reporter
Crane, Derrick, and Hoist Operator
Credit Manager
Custodian
Dancer/Choreographer
Data Entry Keyer
Dental Assistant
Dental Hygienist
Dental Laboratory Technician
Dentist
Designer
Dialysis Technician
Diesel Mechanic
Dietitian and Nutritionist
Dishwasher

132

Dispatcher
Drafter
Drywall Installer and Lather
Economist
Educational Administrator
Electric Sign Installer and Repairer
Electrical and Electronics Engineer
Electrical Power Line Installer
Electrician
Electrocardiograph Technician
Electroencephalographic Technician
Electromechanical Equipment
    Advisor
Electronic Equipment Repairer
Elevator Installer and Repairer
Emergency Medical Technician
Employment Interviewer
Energy Conservation and Use
    Technician
Engineering Technician
Equipment and Vehicle Cleaner
Farm Equipment Mechanic
Farm Worker
Farmer/Farm Manager
File Clerk
Financial Manager
Firefighter
Fish and Game Warden
Flight Attendant
Florist
Food and Beverage Service Worker
Food Service Manager
Forester and Conservation Scientist
Forestry Worker
Forklift Operator
Freight, Stock, and Material Mover
Funeral Director
Gardener and Groundskeeper
General Maintenance Mechanic
General Manager and Top Executive
General Office Clerk
Geographer
Geologist and Geophysicist
Glazier
Guard
Health Administrator
Heating and Cooling Mechanic
Heavy Mobile Equipment Mechanic
Highway Maintenance Worker
Home Appliance and Power Tool
    Repairer

Home Electronic Equipment
    Repairer
Home Health Aide
Hotel/Motel Manager and Assistant
Housekeeper
Human Services Worker
Industrial Designer
Industrial Engineer
Industrial Hygienist
Industrial Machine Repairer
Industrial Traffic Manager
Inspector and Compliance Officer
Inspector, Tester, and Grader
Insulation Worker
Insurance Agent
Insurance Claim Representative
Interpreter and Translator
Jeweler and Watch Repairer
Judge
Kindergarten and Elementary
    School Teacher
Landscape Architect
Laser Technician
Laundry and Dry Cleaning Machinist
Lawyer
Legal Assistant
Librarian
Library Technician
Licensed Practical Nurse
Locksmith
Locomotive Engineer
Logging Worker
Longshore Worker/Stevedore
Machinist
Management Analyst and Consultant
Manufacturer's Representative
Marine Engineer and Architect
Marriage Counselor
Material Moving Equipment
    Operator
Mathematician
Meat Cutter
Mechanical Engineer
Medical Assistant
Medical Record Technician
Merchandise Display Worker
Metal/Plastic Working Machine
    Operator
Metallurgical and Materials
    Engineer
Meteorologist

Millwright
Mining Engineer
Model
Motion Picture Projectionist
Musical Instrument Repairer
Musician and Composer
Nuclear Engineer
Nuclear Medicine Technologist
Nuclear Quality Control Inspector
Numerical Control Machine-tooler
Numerical Control Tool Programmer
Nursery Worker
Nursing Aide
Occupational Therapist
Occupational Therapy Assistant and
    Aide
Office Machine Operator
Office Machine Repairer
Oil and Gas Drilling Production
    Worker
Operations Research Analyst
Ophthalmic Lab Technician
Optician
Optometric Assistant
Optometrist
Orthotist and Prosthetist
Packer/Packager
Painter or Paperhanger
Painting and Coating Machine
    Operator
Parking Lot Attendant
Payroll Clerk
Personnel, Training and Labor
    Relations Specialist
Pest Controller
Petroleum Engineer
Pharmacist
Photo Laboratory Worker
Photoengraver and Lithographer
Photographer and Camera Operator
Physical Therapist
Physician
Physician's Assistant
Physicist and Astronomer
Plasterer
Plumber and Pipe Fitter
Podiatrist
Police Officer, Detective and Special
    Agent
Postal Clerk and Mail Carrier
Postmaster and Mail Superintendent

133

Power Plant Operator
Printing Press Operator
Production Coordinator
Property and Real-estate Manager
Psychologist
Public Administrator
Public Relations Specialist
Purchasing Agent
Radio/TV Announcer and
	Newscaster
Radio Operator
Radiologic Technologist
Railroad Brake and Signal Switcher
Railroad Conductor and Yardmaster
Range Manager
Real-estate Appraiser
Real-estate Sales Agent
Receptionist and Information Clerk
Recreation Attendant and Usher
Recreation Worker
Recreational Therapist
Refuse Collector
Registered Nurse
Religious Worker
Reporter and Correspondent
Research Worker
Reservations Agent
Respiratory Therapist
Retail Sales Manager
Retail Salesperson
Riveter
Road Construction Machine
	Operator

Robotics Technician
Roofer
Roustabout
Sailor and Deckhand
Sales Engineer
Science Technician
Secondary School Teacher
Secretary
Service Station Attendant
Services Sales Representative
Sheet Metal Worker
Shipping and Receiving Clerk
Shoemaker and Repairer
Sign Painter and Letterer
Small-engine Mechanic
Social Scientist
Social Service Aide
Social Worker
Sociologist
Solar Energy System Installer
Special Education Teacher
Speech Pathologist and Audiologist
Sports Professional
Stationary Engineer
Statistical Clerk
Statistician
Stenographer
Stock Clerk
Stockbroker
Structural Metal Worker
Substance Abuse Counselor
Surgical Technologist

Surveyor
Taxi Driver and Chauffeur
Teacher Aide
Technical Sales Worker
Technical Writer
Telephone Installer and Repairer
Telephone Operator
Textile Machinery Operator
Tile Setter
Tool-and-die Maker
Travel Agent
Truck Driver
TV and Radio Repairer
Typist
Ultrasound Technologist
Underwriter
Upholsterer
Urban and Regional Planner
Vending Machine Mechanic
Veterinarian
Veterinarian Laboratory Technician
Visual Arts (Fine and Graphic
	Artist)
Vocational Rehabilitation Counselor
Waiter/Waitress
Water Treatment Plant Operator
Welder
Wholesale and Retail Buyer
Wholesale Trade Sales Worker
Woodworker
Word Processor
Writer and Editor

What Do You Want in a Career?

It is easier to decide what career might be right for you if you know yourself well. You will do best at a job if you work at one that uses your special qualities and talents. We suggest that you use a method called "VIA," which looks at your values, interests, and abilities. The word "via" means the way or the road. Help yourself take the best road to your future—start by thinking about your values, interests and abilities.

What will you value in a job? Do you want to work at a job where you earn lots of money? Do you want to have many responsibilities in your job? The kind of job you look for depends on what you want from a job. List what you are looking for. Here are some things you might value:

benefits	excitement	income
leadership	advancement	training
security	flexibility	power
creativity	independence	variety
challenge	happiness	learning

134

What are your interests and talents? Chances are, you don't think of them as talents. We all know people who are unusually good at music, art, or sports. These are obvious talents. Most of us have talents we don't think about. Are you good at working with people? That's a talent. Working with information and working with details are also talents. Are you patient? Are you well-organized? These are also talents. Are you a good reader? Do you like math? Can you fix things?

Think about your interests. List them. Some interests are used in many careers. Almost any interest ties in with at least one career. Can you think of jobs that are linked to these interests?

skiing	art	cooking
politics	reading	music
teaching	writing	travel
mathematics	motorcycling	gardening

Take a good look at your abilities. List them. You probably have many more skills than you realize. Skills include a wide range of abilities, not just being able to work on a computer, repair cars, or play the piano. Do you have some of the following skills? Maybe you can

manage time	understand quickly
be reliable	motivate people
be efficient	write clearly
be enthusiastic	be accurate
evaluate information	organize well
communicate well	be flexible

How do you use your lists of values, interests, and abilities? Use these lists to help you define what you want in a job or career. Decide if a particular job or career matches your list. You can also use them if you are applying for particular jobs. You might want to make a chart to help you compare several different jobs or careers. Compare them on questions about things you value. They could also help you complete the exercise on the back of this page. It can help you think about what career factors are important to you.

Another way to start thinking about your interests and abilities is to **take an interest and talent inventory**. What's that? It is a pencil and paper exercise to help you think about what you are good at and what careers might interest you. It can point out values, interests, and abilities that you have and may overlook. From your answers, certain patterns of abilities and interests will show. These may match skills used in certain jobs or careers.

What do the scores tell you? The scores do not tell you what job or career you should enter. They simply organize your answers into values, interests, and abilities. Then they suggest careers or jobs in which these interests, values, and abilities are often found.

What do you do with the results? The results give you another tool to use to plan your future and to investigate different careers. Don't just look at the job title. Look at the skills and talents the job uses and see how well they match your own.

Would you like to try one of these exercises? Indiana College Placement and Assessment Center (ICPAC) has a Career Interest Inventory you can use at home. For more information, call ICPAC at (800) 992-2076.

Spend time finding out about careers. Here are some steps to help you get started.

- **Read.** Go to the library. Guides such as the *Dictionary of Occupational Titles* and the *Occupational Outlook Handbook* have lots of information. Some guides also tell you where to get more information. Ask employers for brochures or annual reports to learn more.

- **Talk with people.** Talk with your guidance counselor. Talk with people who work in career areas that interest you. Ask to spend some time at work with them. Ask if you can interview them about their jobs. Ask questions. See if you can tour work sites.

It's worth it to spend time thinking about the kind of career you want. These exercises can help you begin to think about what is important to you. Begin to plan now for a career that matches your values, interests, and abilities!

What's Important to You?

There are many things to consider when you look at career options. This list may help you decide which things are most important to you. How important to you are the following factors? Rank them.

3 = Very Important   2 = Moderately Important   1 = Not Important

_____ **Earnings**—how much the career pays

_____ **Service**—how much the career lets you "do good"

_____ **Interest**—how interested you are in the career

_____ **Growth**—how much the career will let you grow as a person

_____ **Prestige**—how much people will respect you in this career

_____ **Geography**—how easy it will be for you to live where you want in the career

_____ **Independence**—how much the career will let you "be your own boss"

_____ **Security**—how much the career promises long-term, stable employment

_____ **Success**—how well you will do in the career

_____ **Responsibility**—how much people will depend on you

_____ **Teamwork**—how much the career will allow you to work as a member of a group

Which factors are most important to you? _____

_____

Why are these factors so important to you? _____

_____

What different careers or jobs interest you? List three or more._____

_____

What interests you about each of these careers? _____

_____

How does each career you listed match your needs and interests? _____

_____

Which of these careers rank high on the factors you feel are important? _____

_____

136